The RESILIENCE Revolution

Discovering Strengths in Challenging Kids

Larry K. Brendtro

Scott J. Larson

Foreword by John A. Calhoun
Founder of the National Crime Prevention Council

Solution Tree | Press

555 North Morton Street
Bloomington, IN 47404
800.733.6786 (toll free)
812.336.7700
FAX: 812.336.7790
email: info@solution-tree.com
solution-tree.com

Cover Design by Grannan Design, Ltd.
Text Design and Composition by TG Design Group

Printed in the United States of America

ISBN 978-1-932127-82-9

Other Books by the Authors

By Larry Brendtro

Kids Who Outwit Adults

No Disposable Kids

Positive Peer Culture

Reclaiming Youth at Risk

Reclaiming Our Prodigal Sons and Daughters

Re-Educating Troubled Youth

Response Ability Pathways

The Other 23 Hours

Troubled Children and Youth

By Scott Larson

A Fresh Start

A Place for Skeptics

A Way Out

At Risk

City Lights

Doing Time With God

Reclaiming Our Prodigal Sons and Daughters

Risk in Our Midst

When Teens Stray

About the Authors

Larry K. Brendtro, PhD, is former president of Starr
Commonwealth, serving troubled youth in Michigan and Ohio.
He currently serves as dean of Starr Commonwealth's
International Research Council. He is the founder of Reclaiming
Youth International, a nonprofit organization that provides
research and training for professionals, policy leaders, and citi-
zens concerned with at-risk youth. He has worked as a youthcare
worker, educator, and psychologist. He has taught in the area of
children's behavior disorders at the University of Illinois, Ohio
State University, and Augustana College.

Dr. Brendtro holds a doctorate from the University of Michigan
in education and psychology. He has coauthored ten books on
troubled youth, has trained professionals worldwide, and
cofounded the journal *Reclaiming Children and Youth* with
Nicholas Long of American University. In 1994 Dr. Brendtro
established the Black Hills Seminars, an international training
institute for reclaiming youth. Larry and his wife, Janna, a
teacher and editor of youth publications, have three adult children and reside in the Black Hills of South Dakota.

For further information on Reclaiming Youth International, visit
their web site at www.reclaiming.com or call (800) 647-5244.

Scott J. Larson, DMin, is president of Straight Ahead Ministries,
which he cofounded with his wife, Hanne, in 1987. They also
piloted an aftercare home (and lived there nine years) that
housed up to seven youth transitioning from juvenile lockup.

Straight Ahead and its affiliates provide faith-based services for
juvenile offenders in more than 350 facilities in thirteen states
and three countries, as well as a myriad of community-based
aftercare programs. They have also launched a faith- and
community-based residential reentry facility called Straight
Ahead Academy in Massachusetts. Straight Ahead develops
materials, training, and effective models for reaching at-risk
youth for hundreds of organizations around the world.

Dr. Larson has authored or coauthored ten books. His doctoral dissertation for Gordon-Conwell Theological Seminary was titled *The Spiritual Development of At-Risk Youth*. The Larsons are the parents of two children and reside in Massachusetts.

For further information on Straight Ahead Ministries, visit their web site at www.straightahead.org or call (508) 393-7894.

Contents

Foreword

The Resilience Revolution is an extremely important book that addresses the pain felt by delinquent and troubled kids and how society might best respond to its prodigal sons and daughters. The authors delve deeply into history, exploring how we as a society have treated the "problem" of delinquents through our policies and our clinical approaches. This book is a must-read for those wanting to be a part of the solution.

I had the privilege to serve as Commissioner of the Department of Youth Services in Massachusetts and State Chair of the Adolescent Task Force in the mid-to-late 1970s. Our system was reputed to have been the most sophisticated if not the best in the country. We offered roughly twenty-four discrete categories of care, including three levels of foster care and four types of group care up through secure settings. We based this proudly on what we labeled as a "community-based system." Looking back on it, I do not begrudge what we did or how we did it, but my thrust today would be to help structure a community-based system *and* a system of community-based *relationships,* as this book instructs us in how to do.

Some early theorists talked about our lives being spurred either by pursuit of pleasure (Freud) or pursuit of power (Adler). Yet underneath all, as the authors point out, lies a fundamental ache—a hunger for relationship. At-risk kids are isolated, disconnected from family, school, neighborhood, and the social and religious institutions that help bind us to community.

Our youth-serving systems are departmentalized in the educational, juvenile justice, mental health, and social services systems. While we need the best in those who would serve youth, the reigning ethos is to "fix," to keep youth at a kind of clinical arms' length. Even if a childcare worker might want to forge a relationship, caseloads of two to three hundred make it impossible.

We must not be dismissive of those who would fix: We need to understand and untangle the knot of early child abuse. We need the best educators and the best neurologists who can help dyslexic children. But under all of this is the need to belong. In the latter part of the 19th century, Jane Addams asserted that the real solution to delinquency lay not in the courts, but in communities, where caring adults would transmit enduring values to children.

Larson and Brendtro challenge us to develop new ways of connecting to children who seem to refuse to be loved. Most of these children, to whom they have devoted their lives, have been so hurt that they would at first reject the adults who try to work with them. Experience has taught these kids that relationships hurt. The authors surveyed programs for troubled teens across the world, finding that only one in thirteen staff members were really communicating with teens. The rest assumed the role of jailor or administrator.

I write at a time when the United States is locking up seven times more people than it did a generation ago, when more than half of all prisoners are serving time for offenses costing less than a thousand dollars, when almost two-thirds of young adult African-American males will at some time in their lives fall under the purview of the criminal justice system. In addition, there are now more than two million children of prisoners, most of whom are unparented.

Larson and Brendtro introduce us to a stunning and novel concept, namely that the behavior of most troubled youth, rather than being described as "deviant" or "disordered," should be reframed as *pain-based* behavior. Pain drives their actions, not some deficiency in intelligence or character:

- Nick prevents the pain of rejection by keeping people at bay.

- Maria avoids the pain of failure by giving up efforts to succeed.

- Lionel fights the pain of powerlessness by defiant rebellion. (page 6)

The authors propose a new language that is in another sense the oldest language known: the language of forgiveness and restoration. The authors' approach focuses not on punishment, but on resilience, on identifying and developing the child's latent strengths to achieve positive life outcomes. To this end, the authors outline four basic pathways to resilience, four needs that must be met. Every child feels the need for *belonging* ("I mean something to you"); for *mastery* ("I am good at something"); for *independence* ("I have power to make decisions"); and for *generosity* ("I have purpose in my life"). These four constructs echo recent literature on resilience.

In addition to giving some very practical and extremely helpful ways to work with challenging kids, the authors help us blast through the debate on retribution versus rehabilitation. Those who rehabilitate are often caricatured as bleeding hearts, while those who believe in retribution are often painted as cruel and unfeeling. The move to restorative justice helps transcend this unfortunate dichotomy. I recall that in the early 1970s many delinquent kids would say to me, "Yes, I robbed so and so, but I had a lousy lawyer." I was struck by this simultaneous admission of guilt and denial of responsibility. Subsequently I created a program in which youth met their victims in the presence of community mediators. The dual thesis was simple and powerful: "You are responsible for your acts," and "You have the skill someone needs. You can make your life whole."

These authors have given us a gift. Those who work with troubled kids need this book. *Anyone* who interacts with kids needs this book to get down to the fundamental truths of how we relate to the next generation and what it takes from us to be there for all kids.

—John A. Calhoun

Founder of the National Crime Prevention Council
and former United States Commissioner,
Administration for Children, Youth, and Families

Preface

From earliest times, children thrived by connecting to a caring family and community. But in modern society, the bonds between elders and the young have often become tattered. Children weakly attached to adults do not fully learn responsible behavior and values.

If children cannot find concerned mentors or positive peers, they may seek safe haven with other cast-off kids or substitute sex and drugs for genuine bonds. Hungry for respect, many become prisoners to their peers and are easily misled into destructive behavior. Hungry for personal power, they may challenge external authority figures and behave disrespectfully. Some turn inward in loneliness and despair; others become self-destructive.

These behaviors are distress signals that basic needs have not been met. Beneath their defiance, apparent indifference, or reckless bravado, many of today's young people flounder in rivers of pain. Families, courts, schools, churches, and communities could reach out to them, but instead often feel forced to either exclude them or mete out further punishment for their challenging behavior. When their actions bother or frustrate others, these youth are likely to be dealt more pain. This only drives these wounded young people further from the human bond.

Concerned adults need skills to respond to the needs of youth, instead of reacting to their problem behavior. This involves restoring respectful bonds with youth rather than fighting with them. With the support of adults who believe in their potential, youth can discover their hidden talents and learn to creatively solve problems. By developing personal responsibility and contributing to others, youth find purpose in their lives. These skills can be taught to youth by teachers, counselors, parents, and mentors.

And in the process of teaching kids, caregivers can teach themselves to apply these principles and skills to their own struggle with educating and caring for troubled youth. Educators, youthworkers, and parents need to believe in their ability and power to reach all kids, to feel a sense of purpose and excitement about the enormous task ahead. We seek to contribute to that task by writing this guidebook for raising respectful and resilient kids.

We are indebted to the work of many colleagues at the leading edge of the resilience revolution. We dedicate this work to all those seeking to build courage in discouraged children and youth—all those who help kids learn how to recover from pain.

Kids in Pain

Hurt people hurt people.

—*Native American Proverb*

Life has been described as a journey down a long and winding road. The road I have traveled has been twisted, filled with pain—a journey to places most would never want to go.

My childhood was marked by constant trauma. Mom and Dad were always abusing each other and us, too. By the time I was nine, I was put into a class for kids with behavioral problems. If someone tried to be nice, I made an effort, but if they were mean, I let them have it, and in a way they would remember. There were some teachers who really made a difference, but mostly I was such a problem child that the only attention I got was negative.

As a teen, I developed many of my parents' problems, plus post–traumatic stress disorder and juvenile delinquency. The meds I was always on didn't help much, so to numb the pain inside, I cut myself and took illegal drugs. I even tried killing myself several times.

By my mid-teens I had been in countless group homes, hospitals, and programs. I hated being ordered about. When I felt threatened or disrespected, I would act out and make the situation worse. Passed between programs, I felt like a piece of furniture, always getting moved.

My last placement was in a long-term juvenile treatment facility. I could no longer run, so I was finally forced to stop, listen, and be alone with myself, without the aid of drugs or any other escape. I was actually able to listen to people's suggestions, especially those who seemed to genuinely care about me. But they were few and far between. Most of the people who work in juvenile programs are not so polite: "Go here, do this, carry that." "Please" is not often heard.

Eventually, I did my time and left. I was eighteen, that magical age so many delinquent teens look towards for freedom. I was free and they could no longer hold me. But I had never really thought much past that point.

Then I got another blow: "Your brother's dead. A car accident," a caller informed me.

Keith had managed to avoid jail and many of my highs and lows. Why was he dead and I still alive? I had tried to end my life so many times. I would have gladly given my life to save his. But now he was gone.

I made it to the funeral, but I was dead inside. There was nothing left but pain. I had tried to commit suicide many times before, but this time was going to be my last.

Amy's story paints a portrait of pain that is numbingly familiar to other troubled kids and to the adults who work with them. It's a story of mutual frustration. This book is about how to better deal with kids like Amy, how to encourage resilience in all of us so kids don't despair—so that they develop skills to respond to trauma—and so adults working with kids don't despair, either.

The road to resilience, you might say, is paved with trust; the next step is to find the talents and nurture the personal power that will get kids moving on that road. The final "stop" is purpose and generosity, which puts kids in the position of helping others be resilient. We know we have done our work when those we've taught also become teachers.

It all starts with connecting with kids where they're at. And for many, like Amy, that place is a place of pain.

Pain-Based Behavior

In an extensive study of youth in ten residential treatment programs, Dr. James Anglin concluded that *every* young person there, *without exception*, was experiencing deep and pervasive psycho-emotional pain.[1] Perhaps what has traditionally been labeled "deviance" or "disorder" might be better understood as *pain-based behavior*.

This is an important distinction, for as caregivers, we usually find exactly what we're looking for. As long as our attention is focused on the destructive behavior a child displaying, we will conclude that he or she is a problem, based on the pain he or she is causing us. We label kids as disturbed and disruptive if they disturb or disrupt us. But if we can gain a window into the inner world of a youth in pain, we see a very different picture.

Pain is very a powerful motivator that permeates emotions, thinking, and behavior. In Amy's account of her conflicts, for example, she exhibited *painful feelings* of fear and anger, *painful thoughts* that she was bad and unworthy of love, and she reacted with *pain-based behavior* by exhibiting hostility to others.

- *Painful emotions* include negative inner states such as fear, anger, sadness, disgust, hopelessness, helplessness, guilt, hatred, and shame. While there are dozens of labels for negative feelings, most are variations of a handful of basic emotions.

- *Painful thinking* may include distressing thought processes such as worry, anxiety, distrust, pessimism, blame, vengefulness, denial, and inappropriate rationalization.

- *Pain-based behavior* puts painful emotions and thinking into action as an attempt to escape from pain, defend against pain, reciprocate pain, relieve pain, or resolve the problem causing the pain. Acting on anger is the most common behavior, as it appears less risky to a youth than showing vulnerability by expressing hurt or disappointment.

For kids in pain, life is a daily struggle to handle distress and disruption, and they often use counterproductive coping strategies. Struggling to find their way, they exhibit defensive and self-defeating behaviors. But actions that seem senseless to others make perfect sense in the private logic, as Alfred Adler termed it, of a youth in pain.

All behavior serves some purpose, even if it causes further problems. Here are a few other examples of pain-based behaviors of youth in conflict:

- Nick prevents the pain of rejection by keeping people at bay.
- Maria avoids the pain of failure by giving up efforts to succeed.
- Lionel fights the pain of powerlessness by defiant rebellion.
- Ron overrides the pain of conscience by calloused thinking.
- Felicia medicates her loneliness with alcohol and other drugs.
- Ruth compensates for inadequacy by frenetic efforts to achieve.
- Crystal silences the pangs of guilt by inflicting self-abuse.
- Calvin preempts attack by hurting others before they hurt him.
- Lawanda repays past humiliation by joining in ridiculing others.
- Kevin conceals his emptiness by the wild pursuit of pleasure.

Unfortunately, few who work with such children are trained to recognize or address the deep pain concealed beneath defiance or "acting out." Instead, the typical intervention is either a sharp verbal reprimand such as "Watch your language!" or the threat of consequences or loss of privileges. Adults easily become drawn into battles with the very kids who most need encouragement.

The Biology of Pain

When faced with kids who appear tough and threatening on the outside, it's sometimes hard to remember they are still vulnerable on the inside. It may help to remind ourselves that how we interact with each other is affected by biology, not just "attitude." We experience pain in our bodies as well as our minds.

Describing our troubled emotions as "painful" is more than a mere metaphor for physical pain. The phrase "hurt feelings" is literally true. Researchers at UCLA found that physical and social pain operate in similar ways in the brain.[2] They used brain scans to study the reactions of students who were playing a computer ball-tossing game and were excluded by peers. This experience of rejection led to reported feelings of distress and a burst of activity in the area of the brain that processes physical pain and is closely tied to the amygdala, the brain's danger detector.[3]

Researchers concluded that social exclusion registers in a similar way in the brain as the experience of physical pain. Students who were best able to handle the pain of rejection had greater activity in the higher brain, where reason can rein in emotions. The emotional brain can also be tamed when young people use their logical brain to think about or verbalize distress. Thus, talking to a friend or expressing feelings in poetry or diaries can help calm turbulent emotional reactions. As we shall see in following chapters, this creates a powerful opportunity for adult mentors to engage with troubled kids.

Understanding the Triune Brain

Humans have a triune brain specializing in three different tasks: survival, emotions, and logic.

- The *survival brain* is present even in the simplest of animals and is sometimes called the reptilian brain. This, the brain stem, connects directly to the spinal cord and operates biological functions of internal organs like the lungs and heart. The survival brain also executes fight-or-flight reactions.

- The *emotional brain*, also called the limbic brain, wraps around the survival brain and generates positive and negative emotions. The emotional brain is where value is attributed. For example, some reptiles will eat their own young, but the emotional brain would never allow humans to do that. This part of the brain also conditions and stores emotional memories. Emotions motivate, preparing the brain and body for action.

- The *logical brain*, our prefrontal cortex, is the center for logic, language, and reasoning; it also plays a role in regulating emotion. This problem-solving brain lights up in a PET scan when we are thinking or using language skills, but dims when we are emotionally upset; then, the survival and emotional brain light up instead.

These distinctions represent a simplified explanation, of course, as all parts of the brain are interwired in complex fashion.

Neuroscientists have confirmed that the last part of the brain to develop is the logical brain, that region that enables us to manage emotions and to make logical, coherent decisions. The prefrontal cortex, that part of the brain where sound judgments are formed, is not fully developed in most youth until their early to mid-twenties.[4]

During the teen years, on the other hand, the limbic brain, where raw emotions like anger are generated, is entering a stage of hyperdevelopment. This explains in part how teens can be so moody and appear to make decisions driven solely by emotions. Add to that the fact that testosterone levels in boys rise a hundredfold during puberty, and one can see how teens can make imprudent, life-altering decisions with split-second randomness.[5]

The emotional brain's command center is the *amygdala*, the Greek word for almond. The brain has two such almond-shaped structures located inward from each temple. The amygdala is the brain's sentry, our first line of defense. It scans all incoming stimuli to separate threat from opportunity, friend from foe.

The human amygdala specializes in detecting emotional cues by reading facial expressions, eye contact, gestures, and tone of voice. Again, when any potential threat is detected, such as a loud noise or physical attack, the amygdala activates appropriate emotions, such as fear or anger.[6] If the threat is extreme, an *emotional reaction* (ER) can "highjack" the logical brain, and we react without conscious thinking.[7]

The amygdala instructs the brain to record intense events, painful or pleasurable, in long-term memory. If our brains recorded everything, we would be overwhelmed by memories by the time we reached six years old. The brain selects for significance. This is why we are more likely to remember details from emotionally charged moments, like where we were upon hearing the news of 9/11 or of John F. Kennedy or Martin Luther King Jr.'s assassination. Exceptional events and their cues—certain surroundings, gestures, a tone of voice—are stored for quick future reference by the hippocampus, the emotional brain's memory manager.

The next time we see those emotional red flags, the traumatic memory is activated. Sometimes, as in post–traumatic stress disorder, we relive the original terror. In rare cases, when the stress is so overwhelming that we cannot cope, the brain switches course and blocks the bad memory completely.

Thus, children with histories of abuse become hypervigilant, and their brains go into a defensive ER mode at the first sign of hostile intent. The threats they perceive are not only physical; they include threats to self-esteem conveyed by insult or rejection.[8]

This process of building an emotional database of experience begins almost immediately. Even before children can speak, they feel a full range of emotion, from "lung-wrenching anger to limb-flapping joy."[9] By eighteen months, they have the capacity to quickly determine if a new acquaintance is friendly or threatening and behave accordingly. By the time they enter school, most children have sophisticated abilities to detect the most subtle positive and negative emotions in others.[10] Consider how a young child draws a picture of a person: a small body with stick arms and legs, and a big face that reveals emotions through a happy or sad mouth and eyes.

But while children can read the language of emotions, it takes many years for them to learn to manage such feelings. A small child in emotional pain instinctively displays tears or distress. Ideally, caregivers will *respond* to the child's pain with empathy and try to meet the child's needs. But sometimes a youngster's behavior stirs up such distress in us that we *react* in hostility or avoidance and return pain for pain.

Whenever a child's needs are ignored, emotional and behavioral problems intensify. One girl describes her pathway from being hurt to hurting others: "Nobody cares about me, so why should I care about them? I tried to make others as miserable as I was feeling."

Understanding the Tit-for-Tat Rule

Our brains are hard-wired to react to the positive or negative emotions of others in mirror-image fashion. Friendliness usually invites friendliness, while hostility evokes hostility. Psychologists call this the tit-for-tat rule.[11] The principle is simple: *On the first encounter with another person, act friendly. After that, match the other person's friendly or hostile reactions.*

People are by nature highly sociable and seek opportunity for friendly interaction. Tit-for-tat offers a useful means for turning strangers into friends. But cordiality could also make us vulnerable if others have hostile intentions. Thus, humans also have an inbuilt self-protective option.

At the first sign of danger or disrespect, we are biologically programmed to stop being friendly and react with freeze, fight, or flight behavior. Children who have known a lot of hostility are hypersensitive to signs of rancor or disrespect.[12] If they detect they are being disrespected, their private logic can justify counteraggression.

Tit-for-tat is the natural response of the emotional brain to match the emotions we encounter from another. Angry displays of emotion in others trigger anger in us, sometimes in a fraction of a second. Talking to a depressed person can cause feelings of depression in us in a matter of minutes. Of course, positive emotions are also likely to be reciprocated and may even serve to interrupt cycles of conflict. Some may recall the maxim that a soft answer turns away wrath.

We describe this inborn tendency to mirror the feelings expressed by others, as noted earlier, as emotional reaction (ER). *ER Cycles* (Figure 1) shows how painful emotions in a child can be mirrored by the adult and vice versa.

Initially, a child's emotional pain leads to a pain-based reaction. The child's "hostile" display triggers corresponding painful emotions and reactions from the adult. In seconds, conflict escalates as each person mirrors the other's emotions. Once tit-for-tat hostility is triggered, conflict is self-perpetuating until one party disengages or is defeated.

Figure 1

ER Cycles

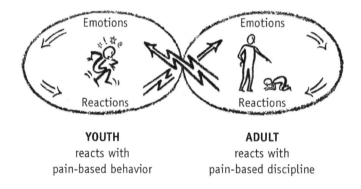

<table>
<tr><td>**YOUTH**
reacts with
pain-based behavior</td><td>**ADULT**
reacts with
pain-based discipline</td></tr>
</table>

While tit-for-tat has survival value when meeting strangers, it is a pretty ineffective way of dealing with troubled kids. "If you respect me, I'll respect you" may sound like common sense, but it backfires with kids who have who have little first-hand experience with being treated with respect.

Caregivers of troubled children are human, too. When we say, "That kid made me mad," we are admitting that we are not exercising logical control over our emotional behavior. We are reacting, rather than responding. Effective work with kids in pain, then, becomes a "double struggle"; it demands that we work hard to respond to the *message* of a youth's emotional reaction, rather than be sucked into our own negative emotional reaction to the angry *form* the message may take.[13]

Dr. Nick Long, author of the Life Space Crisis Intervention (LSCI) model of conflict resolution, uses the analogy of a thermometer and thermostat to describe two possible responses to angry conflict. When the environment heats up, a thermometer simply reflects the temperature. But a thermostat can actually turn down the heat.

Being a thermostat involves learning to override our own innate brain-based programs that prompt us to counter hostility with hostility.

Deficit-Based Thinking

We may also have to override language and perspectives that we take for granted. Often, a caregiver's particular specialty dictates the diagnoses and approach he or she takes in these battles with difficult children. One thing held in common by most theories of response (see Figure 2) is that they are deficit-based, rather than strength-based. We see deficits in the child—deficits of character, intelligence, or behavior—rather than the strengths behind the deviant behavior. We rarely blame deficits in the system or in our own empathy or patience.

Figure 2

13

The Ten Ds of Deviance[15]

Specialty	Diagnosis	Reaction
Parenting	Disobedient	Scold, punish, isolate
Education	Disruptive	Reprimand, suspend, expel
Special education	Disabled	Label, remediate, segregate
Social work	Dysfunctional	Intake, case-manage, discharge
Corrections	Delinquent	Adjudicate, punish, incarcerate
Behaviorism	Disordered	Assess, conditioning, time out
Medicine	Diseased	Diagnose, drug, hospitalize
Psychopathology	Disturbed	Test, treat, restrain
Sociology	Deprived	Study, patronize, resocialize
Folk religion	Demonic	Chastise, exorcize, banish

There is not a shred of scientific evidence that deficit-based strategies build resilient kids, but unfortunately science does not shape public policy. Faced with highly publicized incidents of violence in schools and communities, politicians engage in chest-beating contests over who is toughest on crime. Calls for harsh punishment drown out clear thinking and concern for the needs of children.

How have we responded to kids in pain? Over the past several decades, there have been two prevailing views about how to deal with challenging youth. The first was to punish behavior. The second was to diagnose disorders and to target a presumed pathology with drugs or therapy. On the surface these appear to be opposing philosophies: retribution versus rehabilitation. In reality, both are pessimistic and reactive, focused on deviance and deficit. This contradicts the most basic restorative principles, as well as the science of positive youth development.

Fighting Pain With Pain

To return to punitive control is to admit that we have failed to solve a central problem in education.

—B. F. Skinner[15]

To punish is to administer pain in reaction to undesired behavior. The word "punishment" comes from the Latin word *poèna,* which is translated "pain." Pioneering behavioral psychologist B. F. Skinner recognized that punishment is a failed educational method. Yet punishment remains deeply entrenched in traditional approaches to troubled and troubling youth.

Obviously, to preserve social order, all societies have consequences for serious misbehavior. However, this does not mean that punishing kids for problem behavior will automatically "teach them a lesson," or that not punishing, or using other responses, will necessarily reward negative behavior.

Punishment works best for kids who don't need it, namely those who seek to please adults. But punishment backfires with kids in pain. Why? Because for punishment to be effective, four things are required:

1. The punisher must be able to inflict pain without ill effects.

2. The youth must connect the pain to the behavior, not the punisher.

3. The youth must decide to change the behavior, rather than hide it.

4. The youth must remember the punishment when tempted again.

These four conditions will seldom be met with kids who are termed at-risk, because the bonds between them and the adults who could potentially administer effective punishment have generally been broken. Thus, punishment only serves to further distance the young person from adults.

Yet even youth professionals may view harsh punitive methods as a necessity for those who do not respond to usual discipline approaches.[16] Many also believe coercion is necessary for maintaining order and authority, even as they recognize that coercion does not promote educational growth. Coercive climates interfere with positive growth of all students and increase aggression, depression, and alienation in vulnerable youngsters.

Punitive, coercive strategies are perpetuated by the short-term payoff—a vehicle for venting anger against those who frighten or frustrate us, and a semblance of control in a hostile situation. We need to remind ourselves, however, that when adults become locked in conflict cycles with youth, we are not responding to the pain and needs of the young person. Instead, we are reacting out of our own anger, fear, or frustration.[17]

Our perception of what constitutes a hostile situation is based on more than individual tit-for-tat encounters with troubled kids. Public fear about violence has been hyped by political and media propaganda, even as youth crime has dropped to the lowest level in decades. Demands have been made for punitive treatment of problem youth, and legislators, schools, and parents have responded. Youth in the juvenile justice system are sent to boot camps, ostensibly to learn discipline and respect. Schools adopt zero-tolerance policies to exclude disruptive students. Desperate parents spend enormous sums to ship their troubled teens to private behavior modification camps that have been described as the American gulag.[18] Such programs mask their mistreatment of youth with slick brochures, and some even employ religious language as a marketing strategy.

Violence thrives in these climates of coercion.[19] Once people divide themselves into friend and foe, the tit-for-tat human brain can lead us to commit acts of violence without pangs of conscience. Persons wielding absolute power employ ever harsher punishments against those who resist being controlled. When a crowd attacks outcasts, individuals can be swept along in mob emotion. Submitting to the control of an authority—of another adult, a peer group, or a bully—changes the way we evaluate our own power and personal responsibility.[20] Absolute power by an individual or group is a sure sign that abuse is already underway.

In a well-documented study, Stanford University psychologists recruited normal, mentally stable college students to role-play either guards or inmates in a simulated prison experiment. In only a few days, the "guards" became abusers, and the "prisoners" either submitted to the mistreatment or became violent.

All manner of humiliation and abuse was administered. Prisoners were deprived of most basic needs, stripped naked, marched around with bags covering their heads, and brought to the edge of mental breakdown. The experiment had to be canceled after a week as those who wielded absolute authority became extremely abusive.[21] A more recent example was seen in how American soldiers abused Iraqi prisoners in the Abu Ghraib prison.

While such instances may seem extreme, the same issues are played out on a smaller scale every day, even in our schools. Coercion starts with verbal confrontation and threats. If these do not work, interventions can escalate all the way to physical expressions of violence. In upscale Columbine High, high-status bullies wielded enormous power to make life miserable for outcast peers, while the silent majority of students did nothing.[22] Bullying is not limited to students; teachers can also be victims of verbal or even physical attacks by students. And we have all witnessed teachers who used their rank and power to ridicule or attack students.

Once coercive practices begin, they trigger a collective tit-for-tat: Adults try to coerce youth, and youth try to coerce adults. In such climates, those in authority easily cross the line of abuse, and young persons come to believe they have license to victimize one another. We will never create respectful climates unless we establish an ethos that nobody has the right to hurt anyone else, and everyone has an obligation to help.

The Alliance for Children and Families recently commissioned a study of behavior management methods used with troubled youth.[23] The research identified a potpourri of pain-based forms of discipline used widely today by even well-staffed schools and treatment programs to reform difficult youngsters. The coercive methods fell into three categories: physical coercion, emotional coercion, and social coercion.

Physical coercion: Control is imposed by producing physical distress, as through corporal punishment, physical deprivation, and physical restraint.

For optimal development, children need to know that their basic physical needs will be met. Coercive methods frustrate these basic needs, relying upon physical distress as a means of controlling aberrant behavior.

Corporal punishment, once the mainstay of discipline in both home and school, may include spanking, hitting, hair pulling, the use of pressure points, and other painful treatment. Peers sometimes are given power to punish, and youth may be forced to self-administer punishment by exhaustive exercise, painful posture, or by ingesting noxious substances.[24] Thirteen of the United States are currently under federal investigation for excessively administering these abusive tactics in their state-run juvenile facilities.[25]

In boot camp–style programs, youth are often deprived of physical needs for food, sleep, or shelter. Making physical surroundings austere and uncomfortable is another common form of punishment for problem behavior. Unattractive or rundown surroundings send equally powerful messages.

Restraint and seclusion are common in some educational and treatment programs for troubled children. Humans desire to control their bodies and to be free from physical restriction or confinement, so whether or not restraint is intended as punishment, it is likely to be experienced as such.

There is enormous disparity in the frequency of restraint and seclusion in various settings serving similar youth. Some rarely or never use restraint. But those institutions that see restraint as necessary find it becomes a self-fulfilling prophecy: Once the policy is established, restraint will be needed frequently.

While physical punishment has been on the decline, it has often been replaced by other types of coercion. Studies show that many students experience trauma in school, ranging from put-downs to physically intimidating behavior.[26] At least half of middle school students experience physical harassment or attack by peers. While sixty percent of "worst school experiences" reported by students involve peers, forty percent involve adults.

Emotional coercion: Control is imposed by producing psychological distress, often through forms of discipline that involve threat, hostility, and blame.

Trust is the foundation of all successful work with youth. Threat causes conflict or withdrawal. Examples of threats include verbal intimidation, shouting, swearing, invading space, and menacing looks and gestures. When adults use threatening behavior to establish authority, kids are warned to be wary of them.

Youth need the support of persons who believe in them despite their problems. But fault-finding and judgmental reactions obscure strengths and exaggerate flaws. Blame and criticism are conveyed overtly and by subtle nonverbal signals, such as tone of voice and signs of irritation and rejection. Belittling criticism creates a sense of inadequacy that interferes with the ability to creatively solve problems.

Adults tend to greatly overuse preaching and scolding. Reprimands are the most frequent interventions used by elementary and junior high teachers, who on average deliver one reprimand every two minutes.

While research shows that positive teacher support decreases inappropriate student behavior, such approaches are rare in programs for troubled students.[27] All children need what we would give to our own children: a love that looks beneath problems in search of their causes and solutions.[28]

Social coercion: Control is imposed by restricting normal growth needs through exclusion, frustration, domination, and indifference.

Since all humans have strong motivations for social contact, social exclusion is among the most potent of punishments. Coercive methods that block social relations include lengthy timeouts, rules against physical contact, and the silent treatment.

Most social exclusion operates more subtly, as peers or adults exclude certain individuals from the "in" group. Many of the students who most need a sense of belonging can go through an entire day without any positive interactions with another person.[29]

Curiosity is another powerful human motive, so frustrating normal interests and activities by restricting recreation, athletics, trips, school activities, and even school attendance can be a harsh punishment. Of course, if a youth cannot safely join in an activity, withholding participation is a natural consequence. But systems contrived to block participation are counterproductive with kids in pain.

To gain responsible independence, young persons need opportunities to make decisions and exercise self-control. Instead, many settings stifle autonomy with rigid regulations and adult-imposed routines.

Large, depersonalized schools operate with long lists of prescribed rules and penalties. "But they have to learn to follow rules in life" is a common rationale of those in power. Perhaps that would be true if the rules in schools matched those in the real world. Instead, most are unrelated to the core values we seek to teach.

In an overreaction to fears of school violence, levels of security often exceed supervision needs and undercut the capacity of youth for self-governance. Pervasive monitoring and surveillance limit privacy. Arbitrary reward-and-punishment systems impose order without youth input. But rules not embraced by the governed will be flouted, which leads to only more punishment.

Children who repeatedly refuse to respond to punishment are often subject to the second popular approach to kids in pain: deficit-based diagnosis.

Fighting Pain With Diagnosis

Diagnosing disorders in youth who display troubling behavior has often been seen as the opposite of punishment. In practice, however, those who treat troubled youth as patients or victims share a pessimism on a par with those who favor retribution.

Since much of so-called treatment is nothing more than a variant of control psychology, delinquents do not rush with open arms to their therapists any more than to their wardens. Whether mapped as treatment or punishment, deficit and deviance mindsets lead to dead ends. As with most of life, we get the results predicted by our own expectations: disturbed, dangerous kids.

Two centuries after optimistic reformers began calls for progressive reforms, fewer resources are directed to meet the needs of youngsters with emotional problems. Educational programs for troubled students offer little more than curriculums of control.[30]

Mental health services are rationed due to severe budget cutbacks. In schools and juvenile facilities, drugs replace human connections as the preferred treatment with youth in crisis. Bored students are assumed to have attention deficit disorders when a curriculum deficit disorder diagnosis may be more accurate. Youth in custody are sedated with psychotropic medications, but their mental health needs are ignored, as Amy's story illustrates.

Carefully prescribed and monitored medication can be an important part of healing with some children. But when medications are used to keep problems at bay, only drug companies benefit. Controlling kids with chemicals is a temporary fix; eventually many will go off their medications or mix them with other drugs. And all the while, the core issues that contributed to their pain have not been addressed.

Deficit-based approaches like punishment and diagnosis are detrimental to the healthy development of young people. Rather than pejorative labels that they will absorb into their own self-images, youth in conflict need support—from families, schools, churches, and the juvenile justice system. They need the real deficits in their lives filled with trust, talent, power, and purpose. Instead, they are often passed around the system like pariahs.

Adult-Wary Kids

As a result of these kinds of deficit-based approaches, students like Amy fail in treatment or correctional programs that only manage the outside kid without addressing the hurt of the inner kid. The most "talented" fighters have thick case files that obscure a core problem: These youth don't trust adults. The feeling is mutual. Their behavior frustrates and threatens teachers, who want them removed from their classrooms.

Dr. John Seita, a troubled youth, was kicked out of fifteen court-ordered placements by age twelve. Today he is a professor of social work and noted author on resilience. In *Kids Who Outwit Adults*, Seita describes the strategies used by adult-wary youngsters to deal with distrusted adults.[31] Kids in pain ordinarily turn to caring adults for support. But if caregivers have not been safe and predictable, kids become distrustful.

Fool, Fight, and Flight (see Figure 3, page 22) illustrates three patterns of behaviors that adult-wary youth use to cope with distrusted adults. The most sophisticated strategy is "fool," through which youth skillfully outmaneuver adults and keep them at bay, sometimes even with a smile. "Fight" strategies that oppose authority, on the other hand, express hostility and defiance directly. In a third pattern, youth engage in "flight" by withdrawing from adult contact perceived as threatening or painful.

Some youth have refined a particular strategy to a fine art. But most adult-wary youngsters select from a whole cafeteria of strategies to outwit adults. In *Kids Who Outwit Adults*, Seita portrays this resistance as a kind of misguided resilience, describing how he succeeded at cleverly driving away every adult in his life.

Figure 3

Fool, Fight, and Flight:
How Adult-Wary Kids Outwit Adults

Fool

Denial: *Nothing's wrong. I'm fine.*
Distraction: *The real problem is my mom.*
Confusion: *I'm psycho. You can't help me.*
Charm: *These little talks are so helpful.*
Role reversal: *I've found your weakness.*
Boundary-crossing: *Let's share secrets.*

Fight

Power struggles: *You can't control me.*
Blame: *It's all your fault.*
Threats: *Don't mess with me.*
Verbal insults: *You stupid jerk!*
Battle lines: *You're an adult. You can't understand kids.*
Aggression: *I'll make you suffer.*

Flight

Distancing: *I don't know you, and you sure don't know me.*
Ignorance: *I don't know. . . . Whatever.*
Silence: *You can't make me talk.*
Numbness: *I don't feel anything.*
Fantasy: *I'll make believe things are different.*
Desertion: *I'm outta here.*

© Circle of Courage. Adapted and used with permission.

Stressing Out of Control

As we saw in Amy's story at the beginning of this chapter, young people are swimming in pain. Making the effort not to *drown* in pain creates terrible stress. In fact, the inability to cope with stress underlies most emotional and behavioral problems of children. Stress is part of the fabric of everyday life, but when it becomes too intense, stress leads to pain-based behavior. There are hundreds of stressors that impact the lives of today's children.

Stress in the family interferes with parenting and weakens adult-child bonds. Frequent moves, lack of supportive relatives, divorce, solo parenting, harried work schedules, inadequate childcare, substance abuse, and neglect are all-too-frequent elements of the "deviant" child's world.

School stressors, such as the fear of failure, disrupt learning. Rejection by peers and isolation are particularly problematic during adolescence. Demeaning discipline and simple mismatches of temperament between children and caregivers can also increase stress.[32] The so-called juvenile justice system creates the greatest stress, as revealed by Dr. Anglin's study that showed every kid in the system was in pain.

Tragically, these stressors are coming from the very places that should be providing support. And it's not just kids caught up in the system who suffer. A massive study commissioned by the Carnegie Council on Adolescent Development found that one in four teens is extremely vulnerable to multiple high-risk behaviors, and another one in four is at moderate risk because of excess stress. The report concluded that today's children are susceptible to "a vortex of new risks . . . almost unknown to their parents or grandparents."[33]

Not only are youth exposed to unprecedented levels of stress, stress also impacts them more painfully than adults. Pervasive stress produces pervasive symptoms. Children under duress often display both inner emotional disturbance and outward social maladjustment. They present multiple problems of depression, defiance, school failure, delinquency, substance abuse, premature sexual activity, and sundry rule-breaking and risk-taking behaviors.[34]

A recent study of the five thousand youths committed to Massachusetts Department of Youth Services found that thirty-five percent had been either stabbed or shot. Forty-four percent had witnessed a homicide. And forty percent had been diagnosed with PTSD (post–traumatic stress disorder).[35]

While statistics don't tell much about the inner pain of a child, such data can reveal the scope of the problems we face. The Annenberg Public Policy Center at the University of

Pennsylvania conducted a national survey of over 1,400 mental health professionals in public schools. Respondents rated the seriousness of various student behaviors in the schools in which they worked. It reveals how, contrary to the beliefs of some, serious issues are not isolated to those residing in group homes and juvenile institutions.[36] Take a moment to scan Figure 4 and compare the numbers with your own experience with young people in your school or community.

Figure 4

Percentage of School Professionals Who Rated Issues as Moderate or Great Problems in Their School

Issue	Primary School	Middle School	High School
Mental Health			
Depression	55	57	68
Anxiety	45	45	42
Cutting	10	26	26
Eating disorders	11	13	22
Substance Abuse			
Illegal drugs	25	37	72
Alcohol	12	28	71
Prescription drugs	4	7	23
Drug dealing	9	13	31
Violence and Truancy			
Truancy	50	56	65
Bullying	80	82	54
Fighting	61	57	37
Using weapons	7	5	6

These figures confirm that it's not just troubled kids who are stressing out. If fifty-five percent of primary-school professionals think depression is even a moderate problem among their young pupils, adults have serious work ahead to bring restorative change to all of our children.

Kid-Wary Adults

Creating restorative change in kids will require recognizing our own limitations as adults. Troubled youth are not the only ones who are wary of relationships with others and who struggle with making those relationships work. In the United States, the divorce rate now exceeds fifty percent. And thirty-seven percent of parents of adult children claim they are estranged from at least one of them.[37] Adults tend to be pretty good at initiating relationships with each other, but not as good at maintaining them.

It comes as no surprise that developing and maintaining positive relationships with troubled teens is even more challenging. The result? Fool, fight, and flight are the very same methods most adults use when encountering difficult children, as Figure 5, *Manipulation Antagonism Detachment Disorder*, indicates.

Figure 5

Manipulation Antagonism Detachment (MAD) Disorder: How Kid-Wary Adults Manage Kids

Manipulation
Suspicion: *I can't turn my back on you.*
Secrecy: *I'll never show you my true feelings.*
Deception: *I'll say anything to get my way.*

Antagonism
Fault-finding: *You're just a troublemaker.*
Intimidation: *Nobody messes with me.*
Hostility: *I'll make you pay.*

Detachment
Boundaries: *I can't get involved.*
Indifference: *You're not worth the effort.*
Zero Tolerance: *I'll just get rid of you.*

© Circle of Courage. Adapted and used with permission.

The result is a standoff between adult-wary kids and kid-wary adults. In such adversarial contests, our most needy and vulnerable youth end up as "disposable kids."[38] Frustrated adults *react impulsively* rather than *respond deliberately* to the needs of young people. Such reaction or response is the test of effective or dysfunctional discipline.

Even well-trained individuals experience turbulent emotions when dealing with the challenges posed when kids in pain "become a pain." As one certified teacher of behaviorally disordered children said, "If I had one life to give to my country, it would be Ronnie in the second row."

The Power of Empathy

To be effective, one must override this natural instinct to return pain for pain. Professor William Morse of the University of Michigan often told teachers in training: "The day you forget that, under some life circumstances, you could have ended up like your most troubled student is the day you should quit. You will have lost your ability to respond with empathy."

While empathy is essential, it can arouse buried feelings from our own past, causing us to react in less than helpful ways. Many who want to help others do so because of their own past painful experiences. Previous firsthand experience of pain can become a very powerful tool, when we are able to use it to connect with someone else in pain. In fact, in Latin the word "compassion" literally means "to come alongside with pain."

But as Franciscan priest Richard Rohr has observed, our pain either transforms us, or we transmit it.[39] When adults have unprocessed and unresolved issues of pain, rather than being *wounded healers*, as Henri Nouwen advocated, we become *unhealed wounders*. Nobody benefits when we mirror the behavior of kids in pain. Then we are only giving tit-for-tat, treating others the way they treat us. In contrast, the Golden Rule sets a higher standard, asking us to treat others the way we would like to be treated.

Since problem behavior is primarily pain-based, wouldn't it make more sense to provide children with what they need— what we ourselves would want in their shoes—rather than returning pain for pain? For example, who would punish a child for crying because she's hungry, or refuse to feed that child in the belief that hunger will simply "go away" if ignored?

While most of us accept such reasoning in the case of infants, we worry that it just won't work with older children and teens. So, for example, when a young person who has been deprived of belonging acts out negatively in groups, we react by separating him or her further, and punishing the child through isolation.

Other so-called discipline methods for very young children include putting hot pepper sauce or vinegar on the tongue for lying or sassy talk. Some caregivers spank and hit kids, all the while telling them it's wrong to hit others. Such practices continue despite the fact that punishment has highly unpredictable effects, especially with troubled young people. Often, it only teaches them to become more rebellious, to conceal (to become "sneaky"), or to wallow in self-blame.

When we permit our innate tit-for-tat reflexes to propel us toward punishment, we fritter away our power to create restorative change in youth. These kinds of punishments show a short-sighted focus on changing external behavior while virtually ignoring or even exacerbating the internal causes of infractions. They aim to disguise symptoms of pain rather than heal the wound. They attempt to show our control over children rather than our empathy. They assert adult power to punish bad choices rather than nurture children's power to make good choices.

American educators, parents, and policymakers would do well to study South Africa's attitude toward children. Under President Nelson Mandela, building strengths in youth was elevated to national policy. He formed a Commission on Young People at Risk and set out this goal: "Let us build communities and families in which our children and youth, especially those who are most troubled, can belong."[40] That philosophy has been echoed by Archbishop Desmond Tutu:

> We must look on children in need not as problems
> but as individuals with potential to share if they are
> given the opportunity. Even when they are really
> troublesome, there is some good in them, for, after

all, they were created by God. I would hope we could find creative ways to draw out of our children the good that is there in each of them.[41]

Endnotes

[1] Anglin 2003, 111.

[2] Eisenberger, Lieberman, and Williams 2003.

[3] This region is the anterior cingulate, which is closely tied to the amygdala in assigning an emotional value to stimuli and determining emotional reactions.

[4] Brownlee, Hotinski, Pailthorp, Ragan, and Wong 1999.

[5] Hall 1999.

[6] Aggleton 2000.

[7] Goleman 1995.

[8] Dodge and Somberg 1987.

[9] Greenspan 1997, 49.

[10] Benson 2003.

[11] Rapaport 1960.

[12] Beck 1999.

[13] Long, Wood, and Fecser 2001.

[14] Adapted from Brendtro, Brokenleg, and Van Bockern 2002, 15.

[15] Skinner 1989, 100.

[16] Wood 1988.

[17] Long 1995.

[18] Parks 2002.

[19] Waller 2002.

[20] According to Milgram, submitting to peers or authority triggers "major alterations in the logic system." Milgram 1974, 134.

[21] The tendency of normal persons to become cruel in coercive group situations is described with visual images on Phillip Zimbardo's web site at www.prisonexp.org. For a theoretical discussion, see Zimbardo, Maslach, and Haney 2000.

[22] Brown and Merritt 2002.

[23] This discussion draws from a keynote policy analysis presented by Larry Brendtro in collaboration with Charles Curie of the Substance Abuse and Mental Health Services Administration at a conference of the Alliance for Children and Families in January 2004. The Alliance represents nonprofit children's services in the United States.

[24] Hyman and Snook 1999.

[25] Beiser and Cannon 2004, 30.

[26] Hyman and Snook 2001.

[27] Shores and Wehby 1999.

[28] Benard 2004.

[29] Knitzer, Steinberg, and Fleisch 1990.

[30] Knitzer, Steinberg, and Fleisch 1990.

[31] Seita and Brendtro 2005.

[32] Barber 2002.

[33] From "Turning Points: Preparing American Youth for the 21st Century" (Carnegie Council on Adolescent Development, 1989), as cited in Hersch 1998, 12.

[34] Donovan, Jesser, and Costa 1988.

[35] Suzanne Jazzman, clinical director for the Massachusetts Department of Youth Services, personal communication (November 5, 1999).

[36] APPC 2004.

[37] Taken from general session speech given by John Seita at Black Hills Seminars in June 2004.

[38] Brendtro, Ness, and Mitchell 2005.

[39] Rohr 1996.

[40] Mandela 2003, 418.

[41] Tutu 2002, x.

The Road to Resilience

"Would you tell me, please, which way I ought to go
from here?" asked Alice.

"That depends a good deal on where you want to get
to," said the Cat.

—Lewis Carroll[1]

Jermaine had troubles in school and with the police since he was
eleven years old. His mother was the sole parent and worked
hard at two jobs to make ends meet. Left to fend for himself,
Jermaine gravitated to the street, and his male role models soon
became older gang leaders, who initiated him into delinquency as
a "lookout."

By age fourteen, Jermaine was having both behavioral and learning problems and was expelled from school. Adrift on the streets,
he wound up in the juvenile justice system, shuttled between residential placements.

In residential placements, Jermaine's life actually improved. He
attended school and fed his hunger for positive adult mentors. He

also picked up new skills for turning his life around and a fresh determination to "do good" when he returned to his community.

With each new placement, Jermaine renewed his determination to stay in school and get a job. He really did try. But because of his prior reputation, his attempts to reenroll in school were not met with open arms. Getting a job was not any easier, unless he lied on applications about his delinquency history. Jermaine was just too well-known in the little world in which he lived. His vow to just "chill" and stay away from his "boyz" waned. There was nothing positive to replace the negative trappings of his previous life.

Jermaine had leadership abilities and soon gathered around him a group of a dozen or so peers living in his housing project. Just as he was getting used to the expensive clothes and the clout that being a gang leader affords a young entrepreneur in the city, a clash with a rival gang turned bloody. Jermaine was arrested and charged with possession of firearms and drugs and assault with a deadly weapon. Though he was only fifteen, being locked up was as familiar as home. He knew the staff, the routine, and many of the other residents.

During more than two years in lockup, Jermaine gained more education and counseling. He also became wiser and less naïve and began to lose hope. How could he possibly make it once he was released? What would make this time any different than the past? He knew that the legal consequences of continuing in his actions would be much stiffer once he turned eighteen.

Jermaine's story is echoed in the lives of thousands of today's youth. It's not surprising that an impoverished working single mother would be overwhelmed by the challenges of parenting. It's not surprising that a fatherless kid would turn to older peers for a sense of belonging, or that trouble in school would contribute to delinquency and emotional problems. We know all this.

What we don't seem to know is how to change the script: how to transform a story with "inevitable" elements of risk, failure, and despair into a story of hope. Parents, schools, community members, and the juvenile justice system all struggle to turn the lives of kids like Jermaine around *in time,* while they still have the benefit of the protections society assigns—or should assign—to children. But what works? As we saw in Amy's story in the previous chapter, kids in pain take their problems forward into adulthood. To survive the future, they need to develop resilience now.

The Science of Resilience

The development of human resiliency is none other than the process of healthy human development.

—Bonnie Benard[2]

The science of resilience is a relatively recent arrival on the psychological scene. New studies that chronicle the process by which even our most difficult youth can overcome obstacles and become positive, contributing adults have sparked a resilience revolution.

Resilience is the innate human ability to rebound from adversity with even greater strength to meet future challenges.[3] A leading researcher, Emily Werner, described resilience as the potential to achieve positive life outcomes in spite of risk.[4]

Initially, some scientists hypothesized that resilience was a rare personality trait found only in a few "invulnerable" superkids. But research suggests otherwise: Resilience is the norm. Humans were created with the tendency to overcome all but the most disastrous of experiences. Each of us has descended from ancestors who survived all extremes of hardship. Youth at risk like Jermaine are not doomed kids, not lost causes, not hopeless: Though the challenges surrounding them loom large, they are still resilient kids with unlimited potential.

Studies following children into adulthood found that almost without regard to the risks experienced, sixty percent eventually made positive adjustments.[5] Even children exposed to severe trauma can turn their lives around if they can find supportive persons.[6] Success may not come quickly; typically youth at risk go through turbulent years as teens and young adults before maturing and stabilizing in the third decade of life.

The good news for those who care about kids in pain is that resilience consists of more than an individual's internal strengths. It also includes external supports called "protective factors." The most potent protective factor is the presence of one caring adult in a child's life.

During much of the 20th century, psychology was preoccupied with pathology, and tomes were written about anger, guilt, depression, and anxiety. But after decades dwelling on the dark side of human behavior, a psychology of human strengths is emerging. In fact, as we'll discuss later, strength-based philosophies of youth development have been advocated for centuries.

Studies of strengths broaden our view of behavior problems beyond the narrow psychiatric labels of mental disorders as contained in the *Diagnostic and Statistical Manual of Mental Disorders* (DSM).[7] Prominent child psychiatrists Jon McClellan and John Werry note that only a few disorders, such as autism, fit the classical medical model.[8] The most common problems with challenging young people—anger, fear, impulsiveness, inattention, and moodiness—are part of normal maturation or the result of stress in the environment.[9] Such problems are best addressed by opportunities for positive development.[10]

Sparked by leadership of the American Psychological Association (APA), researchers are once again exploring how to cultivate qualities such as courage, responsibility, and hope. "Much of the task of prevention in this new century will be to understand and learn how to foster these virtues in young people," declared former APA president Martin Seligman in 2003.[11]

We believe that these virtues or principles of resilience can be taught. Each of us has the potential to become that one caring adult in an at-risk child's life, that most potent protective factor that helps hold risk at bay. In an ideal world, however, children have more than one protective factor: They should have a range of external support from family, schools and community, and the juvenile justice system.

Systems in Conflict

A child in conflict needs to be surrounded by a multifaceted supportive community. Sadly, the stakeholders in the child's ecology often operate in isolation or against each other, rather than collaborating with one another and the child. In fact, as Chapter One noted, those potential sources of support—family, school, law—can become sources of the most intense stress. Our kids are in conflict, but so are our systems (see Figure 1).

Figure 1

Systems in Conflict

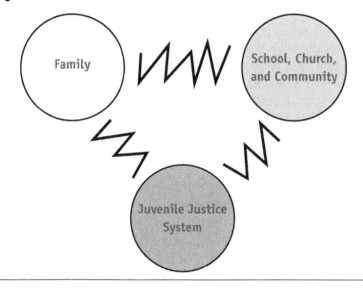

Family

The family is perhaps the most influential system. Every family functions as a complete system—a whole made up of interrelated and interdependent parts—and the unwritten goal of every family is to bring that system into balance or equilibrium. Like an old-fashioned scale, when something is added to one side, a corresponding adjustment must be made on the other side. As a result, individual family members become very adept at intuitively sensing what is needed and naturally fulfilling that role.

We often see how this balance is upset when a rebellious child enters a structured program and begins to exhibit authentic change for the better. No family would ever admit to wanting a son or daughter to remain gang-involved or drug-addicted. But families are generally unaware of the power of a predictable equilibrium. Thus when Jimmy suddenly makes healthy strides, it disrupts the entire system and throws it out of balance. Subconsciously, the whole family works to get Jimmy back into the role he was in before—so that they can maintain their own familiar roles as well.

Those who work in residential programs for chemical dependency recognize that the leading saboteur of all the great work an addict has achieved is often his or her spouse—probably the very person who got the addict to enter treatment in the first place by finally threatening to leave or actually leaving. A wife, for example, after having suffered for years from her husband's addiction, may be the first to smuggle in booze or drugs on a family visit. Why? Because she feels threatened in her role of caretaker. Though she may hate that role, it is at least familiar and predictable; it feels safer than having to invent a new role opposite a husband who suddenly wants a say in how the children are reared and the finances are managed.

It's not much different when a teen comes out of a program talking a new kind of talk. Again, the unwritten goal of every family is to bring the system into equilibrium. In the midst of a crisis, most family members are unaware that they are subconsciously adapting and responding to the actions of the offending member, because the system as a whole seems to be working, based on their previous experience.

Depending upon the extent and duration of the rebellion, one family member might have emerged as the caretaker, while another has become the protector. One has become an enabler, and another has become the forgotten child. The offending child plays the most important role of all: the scapegoat. Without Jimmy or Shelly playing the distracting role of scapegoat, other family members' dysfunctional behaviors become more evident.

When Straight Ahead Ministries conducted focus groups of juvenile offenders asking kids what they felt they needed to really make it, one of their top two responses was, "Work with our families, too." One boy said, "I've been making a lot of changes here, but when I talk about it with my mom on the phone, she feels threatened by it, saying, 'So now you think you're better than the rest of us?'"

It's important for those of us who work with troubled kids to understand that parents tend to sabotage the success of their child if they feel the work is being done without them. Parents want to feel that their bond with their child is a contributing factor to success, not a detracting one. But if we can come alongside parents and support them in what is ultimately their job—to offer their child the best shot possible at becoming a healthy adult—we can forge a powerful alliance. Even when the parent is difficult to work with (prompting that tit-for-tat reaction), we need to remember that it is always in the child's best interest to have family support—and do everything we can to treat parents with respect as well.

Sadly, most schools and juvenile treatment programs focus little or no attention on working with the families of their students, but instead simply cast blame, assuming the family is at fault. This mentality of blame only creates further distrust in those who have the greatest stake in the youngster's success. Parents are the child's first and most important teachers, and even those who are experiencing great problems also have great strengths that can be uncovered if we choose to fight for parents, rather than against them.

Barbara Huff, the founding director of Federation of Families for Children's Mental Health, calls for eliminating the adjective "dysfunctional" as a descriptor for parents.[12] "If you need labels," parents say, "call us overstressed and undersupported." Parents of kids in pain are parents in pain. What father or mother doesn't worry about whether they are "good enough" parents?

Everything we want troubled kids to learn, their parents might also need help with, including self-esteem and problem-solving skills. By contrast, the blame game only sabotages the partnerships that are necessary to meet the needs of children on the edge.

School, Church, and Community

The democratic ideals of the United States once sparked reform in education and the mental health movement. Ironically, the nation known for its idealism has reverted to pessimism about its young. The effects of this line of thinking are only too apparent.

Schools are required to honor the legal principle of zero reject and meet the educational needs of all students. But calls for zero tolerance have led to massive overuse of suspension and expulsion. The formal policy is "Leave no child behind," but the pressure to raise test scores trumps concern for growth of character. A high school teacher told us, "My job is to teach the seventy percent who are good kids. Our school would be better off without the others."

And as we have seen in Jermaine's story, there aren't many second chances for kids who have been expelled. Schools develop policies to keep such youth out of the classroom: One principal told us it is his job to "amputate" troublesome students. Parents of kids in pain may find that teachers and administrators blame them for their children's behavior.

It isn't only schools that let down our kids in pain. Neighborhood housing authorities evict families with troubled kids, and citizens expect police and the justice system to remove delinquents from the community. Most employers refuse to risk hiring ex-offenders, and even churches do not want "bad" kids mixing with "good" kids. Although mental health providers are legally required to have parity with other medical services, managed care has limited treatment to the point that the term "care-less" might be a more accurate description. Prevention is ignored, and serious problems get superficial assessments and symptom management.

Juvenile Justice System

The best evidence that our system fails kids is that most youth placed in juvenile justice facilities are rearrested within just one year of their release. Troubled, uneducated eighteen-year-olds are likely to drift or become homeless upon being cut loose from the final safety net of the juvenile system. Though they may have passed into technical adulthood, their basic needs have still not been met.

Recent decades have seen a tendency to abandon our most difficult kids. There has been a steady dismantling of the juvenile justice system that was created just over a century ago. Juvenile courts were established on the legal principle of insuring the best interests of the child. Calls for "just desserts" have turned back the clock as resources shift from prevention to punishment. The least effective public institution, the adult prison, is used as a depository for thousands of our most troubled and needy youth.

Unfortunately, even in wealthy nations such as the United States, the best interests of children are often subordinate to other priorities. The United States is a world leader when it comes to exacting "justice" through punitive measures. While comprising only five percent of the world's population, the United States houses twenty-three percent of the world's prisoners.[13] In many states, fourteen-year-olds are declared adults and incarcerated with the general population of adult prisons, which violates common sense and international law.

Early reformers who launched a separate court for children did so based upon the commonsense belief that children were different mentally from adults. Their convictions have been proven true through contemporary brain research, as we have seen in Chapter One.

Alcoholics Anonymous defines "insanity" as doing the same thing over and over, but expecting different results. This seems to apply to our current system of providing services for challenging youth. Reversing the impact of decades of punishment and deficit-based intervention will require major shifts in thinking and action. A narrow focus on the problems of youth and their families has blinded us to their strengths and potential for greatness. But in the face of these challenges, there is also a chance for fresh rediscovery of age-old wisdom.

It is time to reject deficit-based thinking and to reclaim the optimism of those who pioneered work with challenging students. Few capture that spirit better than Karl Wilker, who transformed

Berlin's worst training school for delinquents, an infamous institution surrounded by barbed wire.

Wilker's ideas were simple. He demanded that those in authority show respect for all youth, even those who had not yet learned to be respectful. He told his teachers and youth workers to search for strengths concealed beneath problems. And he demanded that all young people take responsibility for their behavior, particularly those who in the past had shown only irresponsibility.

As a result of Wilker's reforms, the worst institutional climate of coercion became a model climate of mutual respect between the young and the old. Wilker attributed this success to a profound belief in the positive potentials of youth.[14]

Reclaiming Our Progressive Past

What we want to achieve in our work with young people is to find and strengthen the positive and healthy elements, no matter how deeply they are hidden. We enthusiastically believe in the existence of those elements even in the seemingly worst of our adolescents.

—*Karl Wilker*[15]

Wilker's transforming ideas were not new ideas. From earliest times, people have wrestled with the question of how to rear responsible, resilient children. Every era has seen pioneering reformers who spoke out for treating children with dignity and respect, and many nations have promoted progressive ideas for working with troubled youth.

Plato argued that teaching respect to the young was more important than giving them riches. But he cautioned that respect could not be taught by reprimand, but only through adults engaged with lifelong visible practice of all they hope to teach youth. Simply, children learn respect by being treated with respect.

Dutch educator and clergyman Erasmus (1466–1536) observed that harsh punishment was a result of adults indulging their own passions, rather than responding helpfully to the errors of the young. In France, Montaigne (1533–1592) proclaimed, "Away with violence!" and lashed out at those who showed no kindness to children, but instead used methods of "horror and cruelty."[16]

After the Napoleonic wars, Johann Heinrich Pestalozzi (1746–1827) of Switzerland founded orphanages for street children. He taught his staff that the biblical call to "become as a little child" meant adults should treat children with deep respect, as equals before the Creator.

These were all minority views in materialistic, dictatorial cultures. The rise of democracy in the 19th century had a profound effect on education, mental health, and juvenile justice. Dorothea Dix (1802–1887) sparked a worldwide mental health movement when she called for treating troubled persons with respect and dignity.

At the dawn of the 20th century, Ellen Key of Sweden (1849–1926) wrote of "soul murder in the schools" and called for an end to demeaning punishment.[17] In Italy, Maria Montessori (1857–1952) railed against "school slavery" and created schools for children from the slums, showing they had highly "absorbent minds." American educator William Kilpatrick (1871–1965) described the ineffectiveness of punitive discipline in schools, and he documented that the average 19th-century Boston school of four hundred pupils gave sixty-five whippings a day, one every six minutes.[18]

In 1899, Jane Addams (1860–1935) founded the modern juvenile court in Chicago. She allied with the Illinois Bar Association to remove children from adult prisons and to provide treatment appropriate to their needs.

Meanwhile, in Poland, Janusz Korczak (1878–1942) founded orphanages for street kids that operated on the principle of the child's right to respect. He called for treating children not as future citizens, but as citizens in embryo. He argued that adults should listen to children and involve them in governing their communities. Korczak challenged the low view of children that was held in both capitalist and communist societies:

> The market value of the very young is small. Only in the sight of God and the Law is the apple blossom worth as much as the apple, green shoots as much as a field of ripe corn.[19]

Soon these progressive ideas spread to all of the world's democracies. By 1928, an international study found that model schools to teach delinquents self-governance existed worldwide.[20]

Unfortunately, few of these progressive ideas lasted beyond the tenures of the reformers. Punitive discipline was still in vogue. There were no formal programs to train new generations of professionals in these progressive methods. Further, there was not yet a solid science of positive youth development. The result was a regression to primitive ideas of treating kids with problems as either evil or "crazy."

Modern society likes to think of itself as civilized, beyond the primitive thinking of the past, but as Chapter One has shown, deficit-based thinking, punishment, incarceration, medication, and coercion are still the most common approaches to kids in pain. In fact, in some ways, the past seems more progressive than the present.

Reclaiming Through Reparenting

What will it take to turn the tide? Sweeping change—the kind Finland recently underwent by closing gulag-like youth prisons and replacing them with innovative treatment and strength-based programs. They exchanged armed guards with caring parent-like staff, and it has worked.

Thirty years ago, Finland had one of the highest rates of incarceration in all of Europe. Today they have the lowest, just 52 per 100,000 people. The United States leads the world at 702 per 100,000, and Russia follows at 664 per 100,000. What is the secret of Finland's revolution? The head of a juvenile facility near Helsinki sums it up like this: "We are parents, that's what we are. And they are pupils."[21]

In depersonalized American schools and institutions, close connections of adults with kids are suspect. But impersonal discipline does not create transformational change. Kids need connections with supportive adults to turn around their lives. In British schools this is called "pastoral care," which means creating a circle of adults who operate *in loco parentis* (in the place of the parent).

Reparenting does not infer replacing biological parents. In fact, as we've already discussed, a child's parents or legal guardians should be warmly welcomed by those who work with troubled kids. Instead, reparenting represents being intentional about connecting to our kids. It reminds youth caregivers to model themselves after the ultimate caregiver of any young person, the parent.

The Circle of Courage Model of Family

The principles of resilience we focus on in the latter half of this book—trust, talent, power, and purpose—are based on the Circle of Courage.[22] Family is essential to the Circle of Courage model of resilience. Larry Brendtro, Martin Brokenleg, and Steve Van Bockern created this model by blending resilience research with time-honored principles of child-rearing in tribal cultures and the writings of early pioneers in education and youth work.

The Circle of Courage (portrayed by Lakota artist George Blue Bird in Figure 2, page 44) identifies four universal needs for children: belonging, mastery, independence, and generosity. When the Circle of Courage is in balance, children develop their strengths and experience positive life outcomes.

Figure 2

44

The Circle of Courage™

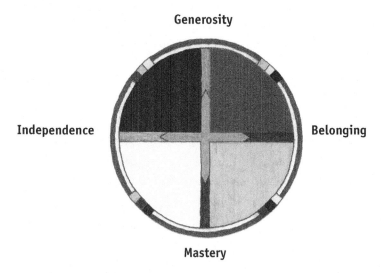

Generosity

Independence · Belonging

Mastery

© Circle of Courage. Used with permission.

Keeping the circle in balance requires protective external factors: the support of family and community.

What constitutes "family" is much broader in the Circle of Courage than in the standard Western sense. Parenting is not limited to biological parents in the Circle of Courage. Indeed, throughout human history, the young were nurtured by extended families, not just one or two individuals. In Native American and other tribal cultures around the world, the family unit still encompasses upward of three hundred people: As Martin Brokenleg puts it, "All of my relatives' grandparents are my grandparents, and all of my relatives' grandchildren are my grandchildren."[23]

The nuclear family is a relatively recent invention of Western civilization. Orphanages are nonexistent in tribal society; there, as the maxim suggests, it really does take a village to raise a child, even and especially in the absence of biological parents. In Western society, however, once the nuclear family is broken, the circle is also broken, and a host of problems emerge. Without the support of family and community to meet their basic needs, children find it much more difficult to develop resilience.

The Principles of Resilience

Many caregivers are drawn to working with troubled kids because of their own traumatic experience or a simple desire to help, but over time, stress can eat away at that inspired initial optimism. How can the educators and youth workers of our time restore their inner conviction that positive change is possible?

In one sense, we must believe in ourselves, in each individual's ability to affect another's life for the better. We must also believe in youth's capacity, with our help, to grow beyond the limits of a traumatic past or a risk-filled environment: We must believe in resilience.

In our work, we outline how educators and caregivers can help troubled kids develop resilience by meeting the four basic emotional needs defined by research and the Circle of Courage model:

- To satisfy the need for **belonging,** build **trust.**
- To satisfy the need for **mastery,** recognize **talent.**
- To satisfy the need for **independence,** promote **power.**
- To satisfy the need for **generosity,** instill **purpose.**

We believe this rejuvenating approach meets important needs for adults, too; we all need resilience in the difficult work of raising healthy kids.

Research Models

The Circle of Courage's central tenets of belonging, mastery, independence, and generosity parallel an important early study on self-worth in children by Stanley Coopersmith. He found that children build a sense of self-worth on the four foundations of significance, competence, power, and virtue, as shown in Figure 3.[24]

Figure 3

Circle of Courage	Self-Worth Research
Belonging develops through opportunities to build trust and form human attachment.	**Significance** is the belief that *I am important to somebody.*
Mastery requires opportunities to develop talent and meet goals for achievement.	**Competence** is the belief that *I am able to solve problems.*
Independence is fostered by opportunities to grow in responsibility and autonomy.	**Power** is the belief that *I am in charge of my life.*
Generosity offers opportunities to be of value to others through acts of respect and altruism.	**Virtue** is the belief that *My life has purpose.*

In the decades following Coopersmith's classic study, the emerging science of resilience reinforces his findings with similar terms for the same concepts. A review of hundreds of studies by Bonnie Benard suggests that resilience is related to four factors: social competence, problem-solving, autonomy, and a sense of purpose.[25]

Additionally, the Search Institute studied hundreds of thousands of children and youth across North America. They identified forty developmental assets that lead to healthy outcomes and build resilience.[26] Half of these are internal assets, such as responsibility, achievement motivation, and interpersonal competence. The other twenty assets are external assets like family support, positive peer influence, and caring school climates.

Figure 4, *The Resilience Code* (pages 48–49), summarizes findings from three other major studies of resilience. Frederic Flach studied resilience in psychotherapy patients; Emmy Werner and Ruth Smith followed high-risk Hawaiian children from childhood to maturity; and Steven and Sybil Wolin studied resilient youth who overcame highly troubled family backgrounds.[27] The results of this mass of research can be simplified into basic categories of trust, talent, power, and purpose.

These detailed findings are consistent with each other and with the broad themes of the Circle of Courage as well. Of course, people are not machines. There is no guarantee that $x + y = z$. But while we can't control the outcomes of young lives, we have more influence than we often realize. Studies consistently show that young people who possess a high number of developmental assets generally turn out well. Those with few assets exhibit many high-risk behaviors, such as school failure, substance abuse, reckless sexuality, emotional problems, and delinquency.

Why do such varied studies reach such similar conclusions? All identify the universal human needs that underlie positive growth and development. When growth needs are met, these strengths naturally develop.

A resilient person is able to form social bonds, solve problems, exercise self-control, and contribute to others. But these are not just abilities: They are *needs* present in all children. They are hard-wired into the human brain, and they are essential to survival and well-being. *We define pain not only by the presence of some traumatic experience, but also by the frustration of basic growth needs.*

Satisfying the Need for Belonging: Building Trust

Every person possesses a fundamental need to belong.[28] This need is best met by frequent positive interactions with at least a few persons who share mutual concern. While rejection produces shame—one of the most painful of human emotions— belonging creates positive feelings and contributes substantially to healthy self-esteem.

Recent studies indicate that the human brain even contains an area for reading emotions on the face, an area distinct from that devoted to the perception of inanimate objects.[29] Laughter and smiling are among the most powerful social bonding mechanisms.[30] As mentioned in Chapter One, tit-for-tat is true for positive responses as well as fearful or angry ones. When the amygdala reads emotions as positive, we send a positive response. From early childhood, we have an innate ability to read visual and auditory cues that tell us whether someone is friend or foe.

Figure 4

The Resilience Code

	Trust (Belonging)	Talent (Mastery)
Flach	A network of friends; a community where one is respected; bonded through humor	Creativity, open-mindedness, receptivity to new ideas; a wide range of interests; self-recognition of one's gifts and talents; willingness to dream; finding novel solutions to meet goals; redefining assumptions and problems to find solutions
Werner & Smith	Caring and attentive family environments; if parents are absent or inattentive, extended family, siblings, and other adults provide counsel, safety, and support; participation in school and community programs	High expectations; academic success; communication skills
Wolin & Wolin	Relationships; bonded through humor; intimate and fulfilling ties to others	Insight, initiative, creativity; taking on demanding tasks; asking tough questions and giving honest answers; bringing order and purpose to chaos

Observe a cluster of teens and notice how smiles and peals of laughter continually punctuate their interactions. Laughter is an auditory signal for bonding, and smiling is the visual equivalent.[31]

Ideally, children meet their need for belonging with a caring relationship to a parent. This forms a basis for later attachments to other adults, peers, teachers, and for parenting the next generation of children.

Humans are remarkably resilient, and when a basic attachment is broken, they are able to reach out to others for substitute belongings. Sometimes this creates problems, as when a gang replaces

Figure 4 (continued)

The Resilience Code

Power (Independence)	Purpose (Generosity)
Autonomy; independence of thought and action; personal discipline and responsibility; insight into one's own feelings; high tolerance of distress; distancing of oneself from destructive relationships	Insight into the feelings of others; hope; commitment; the search for meaning or purpose; faith; a sense of destiny
Personal efficacy; control over one's environment	Empathy, caring; productive roles in family and community
Independence; keeping boundaries and emotional distance from troubled persons; initiative, taking charge of problems; exerting control	Relationships of empathy; capacity to give; morality with an informed conscience; ability to judge right from wrong; valuing decency, compassion, honesty, fair play; responding to needs and suffering of others

family. But strong bonds to a teacher or mentor can also profoundly influence young persons who do not have stable attachments in their families.

Satisfying the Need for Mastery: Nurturing Talent

A core motivation behind much human behavior is the quest to become competent.[32] Children acquire a mass of knowledge, including an entire language code, without formal instruction. The ability to bring all one's knowledge together to solve problems and meet goals through capitalizing on strengths and overcoming limitations is substantially the definition of intelligence.[33] But this ability can only crystallize with the support of adult mentors or more skillful peers.[34]

Research on intelligence has progressed beyond narrow verbal and computational skills to include practical, social, and emotional intelligence.[35] Interestingly, there is little connection between many of these talents and formal test scores. In fact, turning schools into test-prep centers actually stifles learning, says our colleague Linda Lantieri. As Stanley Greenspan has observed, "Letting children know how dumb they are doesn't contribute in any way to making them smart."[36]

In its broadest sense, mastery is *practical* intelligence. It is meeting important life goals by developing strengths and overcoming difficulties. Adults can encourage mastery by tapping the hidden talents in every youngster and giving every child the skills to creatively solve problems.

Satisfying the Need for Independence: Promoting Power

The biggest developmental change as youth approach adolescence is a heightened desire for autonomy. This sparks conflict with adults who still expect youth to act as submissive children. Many behaviors that irritate adults are landmarks on the road to independence.

Children test their strength with loudness and physical horseplay. Teens show bravado and risk-taking and push the limits of adult control. Rule-breaking becomes a practice run at independence. In the ensuing power struggles, youth seek independence, while adults seek control. What youth need more than restrictions are prosocial outlets for their growing need to feel powerful in their own lives and in control of their destinies.

Independent children are not disconnected from attachment to others. In fact, children who are securely attached are best able to develop personal power. Powerful young people feel secure enough to ask for help from caring adults, but also can make their own informed decisions and set the course of their life pathways. They exercise self-control over their emotions, resist negative influence from others, and act with responsibility. They are the pilots of their lives, rather than passengers.

Satisfying the Need for Generosity: Instilling Purpose

For decades, the field of psychology operated as if all human behavior was selfishly motivated, but a significant body of research on altruism shows that concern for others is central to human nature and is foundational for moral development.[37] Altruism has been described as empathy in action.[38]

We once asked teens in a detention center if they had any hopes or dreams for their future. One boy responded, "No. That's why we're here." Kurt Hahn, founder of Outward Bound, noted that many modern youth suffer from the "misery of unimportance" and long to be used in some demanding cause. To find meaning in life, we must commit to a purpose beyond preoccupation with self.

When we have done a good job as caregivers, the youth we care for can become caregivers themselves, and the Circle of Courage is complete.

The remaining chapters present practical, in-depth models for cultivating the principles of resilience in troubled kids and in ourselves.

Endnotes

[1] Carroll [1866] 2002, 53.

[2] Benard 2004, 9.

[3] Walsh 1998.

[4] Werner 1995.

[5] Werner and Smith 1992.

[6] O'Connor, Rutter, and English and Romanian Adoptees Study Team 2000.

[7] The most widely used system for labeling mental health problems is the *Diagnostic and Statistical Manual of Mental Disorders* (DSM)

published by the American Psychiatric Association. For a critique of the DSM approach, see Buetler and Malik 2002.

[8] McClellan and Werry 2004.

[9] McClellan and Werry 2000.

[10] Seligman and Peterson 2003.

[11] Snyder and Lopez 2002, 5.

[12] The Federation of Families for Children's Mental Health is a national parent support and advocacy organization formed by family members of children with mental health needs. The federation has chapters throughout the United States and works to identify problems and solutions to important issues. For further information, visit the organization's web site at www.ffcmh.org. Also see Huff 2000.

[13] Farley and Willwerth 1998, 52.

[14] Wilker [1920] 1993.

[15] Wilker [1920] 1993, 69. Karl Wilker was a physician and educator who transformed Berlin's worst juvenile institution into a model of mutual respect between youth and adults. He wrote *Der Lindenhof,* a rallying cry for the Wandervogel youth movement. When Hitler came to power, Wilker's books were burned, and he fled to South Africa, where he taught in schools for Black students.

[16] Montaigne [1580] 1927.

[17] Key 1909.

[18] Kilpatrick 1928.

[19] Korczak 1967, 468.

[20] Liepmann 1928.

[21] Hoge 2003.

[22] Brendtro, Brokenleg, and Van Bockern 2002.

[23] Presented by Martin Brokenleg in a workshop for families of troubled youth at the Black Hills Seminars in June 2004.

[24] Coopersmith 1967.

[25] Benard 2004.

[26] Search Institute 1998.

[27] See Flach 1989, Werner and Smith 1992, and Wolin and Wolin 1993.

[28] Baumeister and Leary 1995.

[29] Cassidy and Shaver 1999.

[30] Johnson 2003.

[31] Provine 2000.

[32] White 1959.

[33] Sternberg 1997.

[34] Csikszentmihalyi, Rathunde, and Whalen 1993.

[35] Mayer, Salovey, and Caruso 2000.

[36] Greenspan 1997, 213.

[37] Kohn 1990. See also Hunt 1990.

[38] Benard 2004.

Building Trust

Sometimes I say I hate you

because I'm afraid

you don't love me.

—*Theta Burke*[1]

Craig was a youth who had recently transitioned from a secure locked facility to a group home. Having battled adults in the previous program, he continued to set up power struggles in the group home and seemed to be provoking the use of physical restraint. This was puzzling; staff members were not doing anything to escalate physical confrontations. What was the purpose of his behavior?

One person noted that any physical contact was strictly banned in the locked facility from which he came. Perhaps Craig was starving for human touch. Not all agreed, but after much debate, the staff decided to try an experiment for Craig. Certain staff would give Craig appropriate touch: a pat on the back, a "high five" when he had done well, an occasional hug from the side.

Soon he had no need for physical restraint, and all his provoking incidents stopped.

Trust is not some fuzzy feel-good notion: It is an intuitive sense present in every person, forged in experience and hard-wired into the brain. In a trusting relationship, people feel loved and valued. Love—*expressed* in word and action—is the basis for trust. The primary unmet need in most troubled children is the need for trusting relationships.

Pioneers in youth work saw trusting relationships as the foundation of all successful education. In an early text for teachers written in 1829, Samuel Read Hall wrote: "If you succeed in gaining their love, your influence will be greater in some respects than that of parents themselves. It will be in your power to direct them into almost any path you choose."[2]

In 1925, August Aichhorn of Austria declared that love was the secret to reaching "wayward" youth. Then, as now, many mocked this view, calling delinquents "the scum of human society, the rabble that populates the prison a few years later."[3] But Aichhorn saw kids in pain who had received too little genuine love, whether through a lack of kindness or an excess of indulgence. In either case, the result was the same: hatred and oppositional behavior. He set out to build a community of mutual respect.

Early educational and youth work pioneers would be shocked at contemporary discussions about "keeping a professional distance" from "clients." Is the goal really to build walls between troubled youth and the adults they need? Dr. John Seita, a former troubled youth who writes on resilience, contends that the professional preoccupation with maintaining boundaries is often simply a rationalization for detachment.[4] Examples of keep-your-distance mentality abound:

- *Treat them all the same; don't play favorites.*
- *Don't let children become dependent on you.*
- *Those who get emotionally involved burn out.*
- *Relationships risk accusations of sexual abuse.*
- *Discipline requires keeping your social distance.*

While boundaries need to be respected, Seita contends that it is relationships that change people, not programs. Programs only work when they strengthen human connections.

One symptom of the distance between people in our depersonalized society is that human touch has become taboo. We have created a culture of untouchables where we live amidst strangers and ward off all forms of unnecessary closeness.[5] While some children in pain may not respond well to physical touch, all young people need to be touched by acts of kindness that convey they are accepted and valued by others.

Paving the Way

Trust emerges from a secure feeling of acceptance and belonging. In fact, the very word "trust" comes from the German *trost*, which means comfort. We trust those with whom we feel comfortable, those who treat us with respect, and those who help us meet important needs.

The early bonds between child and caregivers create the prototype for later styles of trust or mistrust. Secure trust leads to hope for the future and openness to others. Without trust, children become despondent and oppositional.

In a discussion with a group of troubled boys, we asked if any had ever felt rejected growing up. Five of the seven related memories of times when they believed someone in their immediate family tried to kill them. One boy articulated his life philosophy quite succinctly: "I'll hurt you before you have a chance to hurt me." He said that his most potent memory of growing up was an angry mother shouting, "I wish you'd never been born."

Building trust with kids who have been hurt takes special skill. Such youth often import anger from earlier relationships and target whoever tries to connect with them. As the biology of pain reveals, the brain records all past hurts and sees warning signs of more hurt everywhere. Angry youth have stored a deep database of painful experiences. Those who are most guarded or belligerent are also those who most need positive relationships.

Without a positive connection in the past, kids in pain have no model for relating to others or to their own children in the future. Teachers and others who work with troubled kids have an opportunity to form their first positive bond, to lay the ground-work not just for the present one-on-one relationship, but for future relationships.

At graduation from one of the transitional group homes of Straight Ahead Ministries, one of the students told the house parents what had made the greatest impact during his stay there:

> I had never really seen a marriage up close, so I assumed I would never get married. But after living here for the past year, I decided I would like to be married some day, and I want to have a marriage like yours.
>
> The second thing is that you wrestled with me. My dad never wrestled with me, but you did. If I ever have kids, I'm going to wrestle with them like you did with me.

Committing to Healthy Connections

There is a lot of talk about the importance of relationships, but the concept can be rather vague. In common usage, the term "relationship" may refer to intimate bonds between relatives, friends, and sexual partners. By school age, most of us become adept at forming relationships with peers and adults. These relationships can also be thought of as *connections*. Connections are natural supportive alliances between trusting individuals. Social connections help shape our thinking, values, and behavior. For children at risk, just one positive connection with an adult can make the difference.

Many of those who decide to work with troubled kids know this intuitively. But there is a perception that building relationships is a slow, intensive process. Since busy professionals like teachers serve large numbers of students, they might assume they have little time for building relationships with individual kids. But the building blocks of relationships consist of brief encounters, not marathon sessions. One can have a potent impact in short teaching moments by developing consistent and intentional positive connections.

Humans are highly social beings. We continually scan our interpersonal world to decide whether to connect with those we encounter.[6] As we have seen, the human brain specializes in making quick judgments about whom to approach and whom to avoid. The amygdala handles this security screening by checking out eyes, face, tone of voice, and physical demeanor. Our higher reasoning centers also get into the act by calculating the risks and benefits of reaching out, weighing danger against opportunity. Only those who pass this "trust test" are able to build positive alliances with youth and work cooperatively toward mutual goals.[7]

Some youth respond very quickly to bids for connection, while others may take longer to feel secure enough to overcome distrust. But again, building trust doesn't have to require massive investments of time: Short, distributed positive interactions are just as effective. These give the youth time to "case out" the adult and gain the courage to connect. With cautious persons, attempts to rush to intimacy will be strongly resisted. By nature, we are all suspicious of strangers who attempt to force connections without going through the normal rituals of getting acquainted.[8]

Wary youth are constantly observing adults and making assessments, although we as adults are often unaware of this scrutiny. Often they make a decision in an instant impression of nonverbal behavior, as we all do. For example, college students who rated short silent video clips of professors whom they had never encountered produced similar evaluations as those by other students who took a full semester course from the instructors![9] This underscores the importance of presenting (literally) our "best face" to troubled youth. We need to take a stand of curiosity rather than judgment, and to respond out of a desire to connect with and better understand young people, rather than reacting to whatever behavior they may be throwing our way.

Both craving yet fearing friendship, we all search for clues about those who enter our world. In the end, we make a decision to connect or detach.

- *Connecting*: If a person shows friendly intentions and is "interesting" to us, we are curious and motivated to approach. We exchange eye contact, smiles, respectful greetings, handshakes, conversation, humor, and other friendly bids for connection.[10] If the individual responds in kind—gives tit for tat—we connect.

- *Detaching*: If our bid for connection is met with indifference or hostility, the emotional brain registers a threat and reflects back the same negative reaction. We avoid those who make us feel unwanted or uncomfortable. Based on negative cues in facial expressions, voice tone, or awkward conversation, we conclude, "I just can't connect with that person." This provides sufficient rationale for avoiding them.

Youth who initially appear relationship-resistant have usually learned to fear and distrust adults; underneath, however, they crave such connections. Children are primed to turn to trusted attachment figures in times of trouble. In fact, the very presence of trusted adults or peers greatly reduces the impact of stress.[11]

Kids who have experienced trauma or unresolved conflict are especially hungry to find a supportive listener. As we have learned earlier, the emotional brain can be tamed by verbalizing the feelings of distress. These youth want to tell their story and will likely open up if trust can be established.

In fact, a survey by KidsPeace revealed that most kids would prefer to go to their parents or other adults when in crisis, but often they don't believe they have a relationship that would allow them to talk openly about their problems. So they go to their friends first, but only as their second choice.[12]

Straight Ahead Ministries recently conducted several focus groups with troubled students to find what they felt they most needed to succeed in life. The number one factor cited was having a positive, trusting connection with the adults working with them.

When asked what kind of actions would indicate that an adult cared, they gave the following responses:

- *We all have lots of problems, but when we know adults want to help us instead of just seeing us as their job, we can take the risk to change.*

- *Remembering things about me or what I've told you let's me know you care and that you listen to me.*

- *Keep promises that you make.*

- *Just showing up when you're supposed to says that I mean something to you.*

- *Spending time with us makes me feel we matter.*

One boy simply responded, "Tell us you're glad that we're here."

The Need for Mentors on the Journey

Among the most potent relationships for positive youth development are those provided by mentors. The term "mentor" comes from the *Odyssey* by Homer: When Odysseus sought a wise counselor for his young son, Telemachus, he chose Mentor, a person he trusted and valued highly. A mentor is any person who teaches, guides, and inspires a young person in a caring and mutually satisfying relationship.[13] Mentors, then, can be teachers, counselors, relatives, adult volunteers, or responsible peers.

As mentioned previously, not until the past several decades in Western culture was the job of rearing healthy children given solely to one or two biological parents. With the breakdown of extended families and strong communities came a much more individualized approach to rearing children. This is a bold contrast to the natural interrelatedness of neighbors and relatives that marked less transient neighborhoods and still exists in simpler tribal cultures.

In recent years, the concept of mentoring has resurfaced as a way to fill a much-needed void in raising healthy children. But while formal mentoring programs may work well with children and younger adolescents, few older teens are looking for a "big brother" or "big sister" (the popular images of a mentor). Ask yourself: "Have any of my closest friends come by being assigned to me in a formal program?"

The need for mentors among older adolescents is undeniable, but the key to fostering such relationships is to create natural environments where youth and adults can begin to connect with one another. We like to use the image of a three-legged stool as we think through mentoring programs with teens (see Figure 1).

- The first and strongest leg is an *adult* who has the desire and training to be a mentor. Not everyone who expresses interest in mentoring is a good candidate, however. If an adult wants to mentor out of a personal need for significance or accomplishment, kids quickly sniff that out and often work to sabotage the relationship. No one likes to be another person's project. The most effective mentors just want to be with kids on the journey and are flexible regarding the destination.

- The second leg of the stool is the *young person*. This is generally the shakiest leg, since teens in trouble often have not had many positive adult bonds. Yet for that very reason, they are silently starving for connections, which is why they often seek out de facto mentors in gangs or exploitative relationships.

- The third leg is the *setting*. Schools, churches, neighborhoods, and youth programs provide natural settings for connections to occur. In some programs, youth are assigned mentors, but the more natural the setting, the better.

"Hi, I'd like to be your mentor" will drive most kids away—or anybody, for that matter. Research shows that mentors who try to frontally build relationships—to circumvent the brain's natural tendency to evaluate strangers as friend or foe—are less likely to connect than those who take their cue from the youth. When we respond to a youth's needs, connections naturally follow. Thus, mentoring requires some setting that allows adults to connect in a shared activity, interest, or task.

Figure 1

Key Aspects of a Teen Mentoring Program

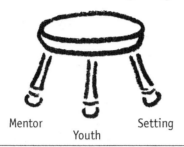

Mentor   Setting

Youth

In our experience, unless two of the three legs of the stool are solid, the mentoring relationship will have little chance for success. Because we can assume the youth might be fairly unstable, the real challenge is in making the other two legs as strong as possible by providing kids with competent mentors in supportive settings. As those elements are strengthened, the young person becomes stronger as well.

Schools can provide both structured and spontaneous opportunities for adults to interact with youth, although many educators are uncomfortable operating outside their formal roles. Those untrained to talk with kids in conflict are likely to retreat from problems or revert to moralistic, authoritarian methods. Some teaching roles lend themselves especially well to building strong connections, such as coaching and the arts. Many schools have also added after-school programs, which offer a more friendly setting for cross-generational connections.

When youth are living in a residential program or mandated to report to a community center, these settings can also serve as a stable third leg, simply because youth are going to be there already. If a program is offered on Wednesday evening from 7:00–8:00 p.m., there is a good chance that kids will attend if it meets their needs or desires.

Straight Ahead Ministries and its affiliates offer Bible discussion groups led by local volunteers in hundreds of juvenile facilities across the country. Typically, thirty-five to forty percent of the youth choose to attend. This can be the first step in forging meaningful mentoring relationships.

On the other hand, programs that are not voluntary are apt to backfire. One juvenile facility decided to make Straight Ahead's faith-based "recovery" program mandatory and assigned half of the thirty-six girls in the facility to attend. The girls had horrible attitudes about being there and refused to engage in any meaningful dialogue.

"Why was I picked for this group?" some complained, saying, "Other girls in here got lots more issues than me, so why don't they have to come?!" When the program was converted to a voluntary basis, all but three of the thirty-six girls in the facility signed up.

Another way to create a strong third leg of the stool is by asking youth what *they* feel they need or want, and then providing places and activities to meet that need. Before starting any new initiative, Straight Ahead Ministries goes through the process of conducting focus groups with kids, asking what they feel they need and then designing the program with that in mind. Many adults are surprised that getting a job and receiving an education rate higher than recreation among most young offenders trying to change the course of their lives.

A good question to ask before launching a mentoring program is, "Where are teens already currently gathering in our community?" Consider offering the program there, rather than trying to get them to come to a place where you think they should congregate. In Europe, many youth workers operate out of mobile vans so they can seek out at-risk youth on their natural turf, even if it's a park or train station.

However the program is structured, a primary value of mentors is to help youth gain more creative problem-solving skills than would be possible by acting alone. Mentors need not be exclusively adults. Youth are eager to model the behavior of slightly more mature young persons, so capable peers can also provide much needed support and guidance.[14]

And mentoring need not be only a one-to-one relationship. Studies have shown that group mentoring is just as powerful, especially with older teens. This can happen with one adult and three or four young people, or with two or three adults engaging on a regular basis with six to eight youth, especially around a project like community service.

One reason mentoring connections are effective, however the relationship is structured, is that they operate through the power of trust, rather than coercion.

Some years ago, state officials were concerned that Straight Ahead Ministries' aftercare home was housing too many youth with high-profile cases. At the time, four of the six residents had manslaughter charges on their records. Officials wanted to change the structure of the home. They wanted overnight-shift staff to monitor the kids while they were sleeping and to have their doors alarmed—even though this was an aftercare home, where youth chose to live after they had completed their sentence.

"The only things we have to hold these kids are trust and relationships," staff said. "They have already made the hard choice to come here when they weren't required to do so, and if we turn the house into just another 'program,' most wouldn't choose to be here. Dismantling the feeling of family in exchange for an us-versus-them climate would actually make it *less* safe." The state relented, and the aftercare home and the kids in it continued to flourish.

Whether in a school or in a secure facility, the environment is only as safe as the trust that exists within that community. Attempts to beef up security in schools and elsewhere only fuel young peoples' distrust of those in authority, especially those who assume the worst about their charges, react out of fear, and apply coercive controls.

Strategies for Connecting

Mountains of files document failed interventions with "incorrigible" youth who "can't be trusted." Rather than writing these kids off, what if we viewed their resistance as evidence that they still believe adults are not acting in their best interests?[15] And what if we were determined to prove otherwise?

Social bonds are on the line in every interpersonal encounter.[16] If we do not actively build or repair connections, we allow them to inevitably weaken and deteriorate. Problems pose powerful opportunities for teaching and connecting, so it is ironic that traditional discipline cuts off positive communication with punishment and coercion at the very time youth need love and support.

Some worry that giving "attention" to kids who are misbehaving will reward problem behavior. While that is possible, the reality is usually quite different. Providing support in moments of crisis actually serves to strengthen connections and coping skills. If we want to help children with their problems, we must prove that *we* can be trusted—to respond, not to react. We need methods of securing voluntary cooperation from kids so that we don't get drawn into adversarial contests.

Tell One on Yourself

One of the most powerful means of building trust with kids in pain is the appropriate sharing of our own related stories. "Telling one on yourself" forges a powerful connection and sets the bar for a deeper level of communication.

Traditional counseling training forbids personal disclosure on the part of the adult, but maintaining such a guarded distance does little to break down walls of hurt and mistrust. In tit-for-tat fashion, we show trust to persons who show trust to us. We are also guarded to those who are guarded with us.

If we are going to effectively support a youth in crisis, it helps if that person knows we have an idea of what he or she is experiencing. Someone once said, "If you are going to take someone to the edge of despair, you must at least be willing to hold their hand." Sharing similar situations from our own experience can be an exercise in handholding, as long as we don't dwell on our story.

For example, when Robin Williams' character in the movie *Good Will Hunting* briefly notes how he felt when his drunken father came home and beat him as a child, he makes a powerful connection and provides a safe place for Will Hunting to go deeper in telling his own story.[17]

One way to gauge when personal disclosure may be manipulative or an exercise in one-upmanship is to continually ask oneself, "Am

I telling this story for my sake or for the sake of the young person?" The latter must always be the case for it to be helpful.

The adult must also have some distance from and resolution of the particular area of pain for it to be shared in a healthy way. But part of the definition of empathy is the ability to reach inside one's own area of resolved pain to touch another at their point of pain.

Sharing experience forges a connection to a child who feels isolated by pain. Judiciously applied, "telling one on yourself" encourages the child to keep talking about his or her own experience, and to even go deeper.

Apply Verbal Judo

Another promising strategy for connecting with troubled kids is *verbal judo,* developed by George Thompson, a communications professor turned cop.[18]

The Japanese word "judo" is a combination of *ju*, meaning "gentle," and *do*, which means "way." Thus, judo means the gentle way. When Thompson first became a police officer, he got into frequent physical confrontations because he expected to be treated with respect and would take no nonsense or abuse. In time, he learned the power of taking abuse and disrespect with dignity and style.

In verbal judo, one responds to hostility with communication, rather than reacting with force. This does not mean telling people who are upset to "calm down," since such criticism implies that they have no right to be upset.

Thompson believes that the best response to angry people is to accept their angry feelings, while at the same time trying to shape a positive outcome. Thus, anger can be met with a comment like, "I hear what you're saying, so how can we solve this problem?"

The most effective methods of changing behavior involve providing encouragement, raising questions, and helping youth clarify and reframe the problems they are facing.[19] Even when discussing problems, we have opportunities to validate the positive qualities of young persons. Instead of a blaming question like, "Why did you do something like that?" we can ask, "How did a great kid like you get into that kind of trouble?" This conveys that the youth is more than his or her behavior.

By having and showing respect and empathy, we remain calm in the midst of conflict and deflect verbal abuse. Without genuine empathy, there is little likelihood an upset person will listen to us, no matter what we say. We communicate far more through our way of being than through mere words.

It is not what we *say* that is ultimately communicated, but what others *experience* from us. As mentors and caregivers, we must be continually working through our own issues, especially as they become heightened by the actions of an angry young person, for it is nearly impossible to mask what is in the heart.

Turn Rancor to Respect

Swiss psychologist Paul Diel[20] observed that verbal or nonverbal rancor was among the most destructive forces to relationships. Rancor is an emotionally charged communication that conveys bitterness and malice. This is the most easily spotted symptom of discord in any relationship. In Malcolm Gladwell's book *Blink*, scientists studying marital relationships call this concept "contempt" and consider it a "fatal" sign of a relationship beyond repair.[21] Diel's first step in work with families or other adults, however, was to get them to immediately cease any rancor and reproach.

If we intend to connect with youth, we must also become aware of our own specific behaviors that destroy connections. Rancor is conveyed in verbal and nonverbal signals, both overt and subtle. Examples include demeaning words or even neutral speech delivered with sarcasm and innuendo. Hostile stares, smirks, and rolling eyes convey rancor and sabotage efforts at connection.[22] But signs of respect send the message, "It is safe to connect. You won't be hurt or ridiculed."

Whether dealing with youth or adults, the goal is to replace rancor with respect—in ourselves and the other person. An interesting exercise is to take the list of characteristics of rancor and respect (Figure 2) and use it to evaluate a few minutes of interactions on

some controversial news panel or debate. The tone of this adult
interaction is likely to be highly disrespectful.

Figure 2

Characteristics of Rancor and Respect

Rancor	Respect
Hostile	Friendly
Blaming	Empathizing
Demeaning	Encouraging
Impatient	Patient
Arrogant	Humble
Dominating	Empowering
Indifferent	Interested
Provocative	Calming
Argumentative	Cooperative
Vengeful	Forgiving

When we prepare teachers to work with troubled youth, we
encourage them to learn to monitor their own rancor in tense
encounters with kids. Ask yourself: "Would I speak to my super-
visor or a respected friend in this tone of voice?"

It is normal for rancor to bubble to the surface when we are
stressed or irritated. If we feel rancor in ourselves, the youth is
likely similarly disposed. So when we spot rancor in our own interactions, it is advisable to take a deep breath and change our tone.

The fact that a kid angered us can even be useful information.
We learn important lessons from kids who resist and refuse to
cooperate: They are actually teaching us that there are better
ways of connecting with them.[23] If we did nothing to provoke a
negative response, then we still have learned that these are feelings this kid typically stirs in others as well.

Even if we have to be very firm, as when a teacher takes control
of an unruly group, it is best done without a tone of rancor or
defensiveness, but rather with a professional demeanor of being
securely in charge. The only way to demand this kind of respect
is by giving it.

Chapter Three Building Trust

Just treating kids well does not mean they will instantly return the favor. Some might even initially misinterpret respect as weakness. We must not take resistance as a personal attack, but get busy figuring out how to motivate the youth to be more responsive and respectful. This ordinarily starts with us modeling this behavior for them.

What does respect look like to kids? In a formal study, young persons evaluated video clips of interactions between adults and youth.[24] They were asked to rate behaviors that they most liked and disliked (see Figure 3). Researchers used the results to train persons to work with troubled youth. They were surprised to discover that joking, among the most highly rated of behaviors, was almost nonexistent in structured adult-supervised settings.

Figure 3

Adult Behaviors Ranked by Youth: Scale of 0 (Worst) to 4 (Best)

Rancor From Adults *Behaviors That Youth Dislike*		Respect From Adults *Behaviors That Youth Desire*	
Throwing objects	0.0	Calm, pleasant voice	3.8
Accusing or blaming	0.1	Offering to help	3.7
Shouting	0.1	Joking	3.6
No opportunity to speak	0.3	Positive feedback	3.6
Mean, insulting remarks	0.5	Fairness	3.6
Negative physical contact	0.6	Explaining how and what	3.4
Bad attitude	0.6	Politeness	3.3
Bossy or demanding	0.7	Getting right to the point	3.1
Unpleasant	0.8	Smiling	3.0
Unfriendly	0.9		
Lack of understanding	1.0		
Profanity	1.0		

Recalling our discussion of the brain, rancor triggers negative emotions, while respect activates positive emotions. Respectful adults become attractive role models to youth, particularly those who have experienced hostility from other authority figures.

Still, many adults assume they must use intimidating behavior to exercise authority. In fact, such behaviors put youth and adults into warring camps.

The Resilience Revolution

Wait, Listen, and Learn

It is important to reiterate that youth who initially appear relationship-resistant have usually learned to fear and distrust adults, but underneath they crave such connections. Russell was one such sixteen-year-old that we met under odd circumstances. His grandmother brought him in tow to a workshop we were leading for alternative schools working with at-risk youth.

She introduced him to us and said, "Please talk to him; this boy has caused me more trouble than all my sons put together. He got kicked out of school and is in an alternative school, but he hates it. He won't talk to his counselor from the court, either."

Russell initially appeared uncomfortable as the only youth in attendance. Between sessions, we used humor to engage him in brief interactions, making sure not to become pushy and drive him away. As the two-day workshop proceeded, he and his grandmother moved closer to the front row.

Russell was intrigued by the discussion of why adults have difficulty connecting with kids, and he volunteered examples from his own experiences. He was well-received and formed many positive connections at the workshop. Here are some of the comments he shared:

> Counselors try to talk to me, but don't set up a comfort zone. They just dive in and probe for information. They're perfect strangers, so why should I give them my life history? I just tell them what they need to know.

> Adults shouldn't be afraid to be friendly and tell a little about themselves and why they want to help kids. Some adults set themselves above kids. They lay down the law: "You do what I say when I say it!" or "Don't get up without my permission."

> They would get better results if they would say, "I'd appreciate it if you would help me figure out what you want to happen in your life." Kids listen to adults who listen to them.

When one looks beneath the behavior of adult-wary kids, a much different picture emerges. Though they may keep us at bay, these young persons are hungry to connect to those who pass the trust test. *Tips for Building Trust* (Figure 4) provides a list of practical strategies for building connections to adult-wary kids.[25]

Figure 4

Tips for Building Trust

1. Turn problems into learning opportunities.
   Please coach me. Don't scold me.
2. Provide fail-safe relationships.
   A person like me really needs a fan club.
3. Increase dosages of nurturance.
   I need to believe that you really care.
4. Don't crowd.
   When you get too close, I will back away for a while.
5. Use the back door.
   If you help me do well in something important to me, you are important to me.
6. Decode the meaning of behavior.
   I try to hide what I really think.
7. Be authoritative, not authoritarian.
   Don't control me. Help me to control myself.
8. Model respect to the disrespectful.
   Your respect helps build mine.
9. Enlist youth as colleagues.
   I am the only real expert on myself.
10. Touch in small ways.
    I watch little things you do to discover who you are.
11. Give seeds time to grow.
    Please be patient with me—I am still learning.
12. Connect youth to cultural and spiritual roots.
    I need to know there is a purpose for my life.

© Circle of Courage. Used with permission.

Putting Ourselves to the Test

We asked groups of students in two high schools to help us develop a rating scale that those who work with youth could use to see if they were really building trusting connections with kids. The youth had many suggestions, which were distilled into the accompanying list of ten questions (Figure 5, page 74) for adults to use in rating themselves.

We presented the rating scale designed by the students to their teachers. Most were intrigued, but found the directions challenging: *They were to score themselves according to how they felt their students would rate them, not how they would rate themselves.*

In a discussion at one school, there was a consensus among the faculty that young people have very high expectations of adults in their lives. Yes, they do, but would we want it any other way? After all, if it's kids we are called to teach, and not mere material, any input they can give us is to our benefit. They can teach us, too. As we shall see in the next chapter, troubled young people have their own knowledge and talents to share.

74

An Exam for Those Who Teach

Please circle how you think the young persons you work with would rate you.

		Never		Often		Always
1. I listen to young persons.		1	2	3	4	5
2. I respect kids as I do adults.		1	2	3	4	5
3. I set high expectations.		1	2	3	4	5
4. I try to help all kids succeed.		1	2	3	4	5
5. I am friendly to young people.		1	2	3	4	5
6. I model the behavior that I expect.		1	2	3	4	5
7. I am fair and don't play favorites.		1	2	3	4	5
8. I am careful not to embarrass kids.		1	2	3	4	5
9. I always use a respectful tone.		1	2	3	4	5
10. I keep trying with difficult kids.		1	2	3	4	5

Total your score and multiply by 2 to find your percentage
_____ x 2 = _____ %

Scoring: Give yourself an A if you scored 90% or higher; B for 80–89%; C for 70–79%; D for 60–69. If you scored below 59%, give yourself an F.

Endnotes

[1] Burke 1976, 4.

[2] S. R. Hall [1829] 1973, 47.

[3] Pfister 1956, 40.

[4] Seita and Brendtro 2005.

[5] Montague and Matson 1979.

[6] Humans can even make connections to other species because of the mutual interest certain "tame" mammals have in one another. Thus, pets can become very loyal and serve as substitutes for supportive human connections.

[7] Kozart 2002.

[8] De Becker 1998.

[9] Gladwell 2005, 12–13.

[10] Gottman 2001.

[11] Lynch 1977.

[12] KidsPeace 1998.

[13] Treffinger 2003.

[14] Vygotsky 1989.

[15] Anglin 2003.

[16] Scheff 1995.

[17] Van Sant 1998.

[18] Thompson and Jenkins 1993.

[19] Dishion and Kavanagh 2003.

[20] Diel 1987.

[21] Gladwell 2005.

[22] Patterson 2002a. See also Gottman 2001.

[23] Blanchard 1995.

[24] Willner et al. 1970.

[25] Adapted from Seita and Brendtro 2005.

chapter four

Nurturing Talent

The very qualities of sagacity and daring which formerly rendered them a terror to the community will push them forward in their new career of virtue, honor, and usefulness.

—S. D. Brooks, 1856[1]

We once asked a group of kids we had been working with at a detention center, "What would you like to be doing in five years?"

It was a shift from the typical conversation they had been engaged in, a conversation that usually focused on what they were doing wrong and what wasn't working. They had become pretty clear on what they didn't want, but being asked to examine what they did want posed a new, greater dilemma.

None of the kids wanted to respond. They had been in and out of institutions so many times, and each had made countless promises that this would be their last time in lockup. Their reluctance to make yet another empty promise lingered heavy in the air. The pain of disappointment, of hopes being raised and then dashed, was more painful than the acceptance of failure, even inevitable failure.

Finally Luis took the courageous step to put into words what was obviously being felt by all: "I'll be in prison in five years."

"Why do you say that?" we challenged him. "You'll be out of here in a couple of months."

He shrugged. "'Cause I've always been a troublemaker and I'll always be a troublemaker."

How many times must Luis have heard such things said about himself? By fifteen, that sense of failure had become part of his very identity. Kids like Luis have experienced so much failure in their young lives that they begin to feel more comfortable failing than they do succeeding. Success is scary. Failure is at least familiar.

Even when accomplishments come, troubled kids find it hard to accept them. Recently we spoke with a boy who was back in detention, where we had seen him many times over the past three years. "What happened?" we asked.

"I don't know. I guess I was just doing *too* good," he responded. "I was back in school, I had a job, and things were really coming together. My family was proud of me for the first time I can remember. Then I started getting scared. I knew I wouldn't be able to keep it up. Eventually I was going to crash and disappoint everybody, so I figured I might as well just do it now, before I had too much to lose."

Failure complexes run deep. When a person has known only failure, each new challenge becomes a threat: of more frustration, more pain, the same old cycle of despair. Kids who have failed in the past assume the worst about their own potential and no longer believe they can succeed at anything. One of the most common tattoos worn by young men in prisons today is simply "Born to Lose."

Mapping Talents

Resilience involves the ability to solve problems by developing strengths and overcoming difficulties. A deficit-based perspective, which is the substance of most work with troubled kids, does nothing to aid in the development of resilience. Looking back on his own troubled youth, John Seita recalls that the adults who made a difference in his life conducted "talent hunts" to find his hidden potential. Today, as a youth development expert, he is not surprised to find that most kids—including those who are apparently well-adjusted—have great difficulty identifying their strengths and talents.

Talent, as we're describing it here, involves both the unique learning styles and abilities present in every person as well as problem-solving skills, which are foundational to success in academics, the arts, athletics, interpersonal relationships, and every other area of life. Troubled children often face special difficulties in recognizing and developing their talents in school, but they also struggle to develop interpersonal and problem-solving skills. As time passes, these problems feed into each other and create the deep sense of failure we see in kids like Luis.

In the 1960s, when the field of learning disabilities was emerging, the prevailing approach was to diagnose the learning deficit in a student, and then spend hours and hours trying to remedy that flaw. Occasionally it worked, but more often it wasted time. It was like asking a child with a hopelessly withered arm to make that limb as powerful as his healthy arm—an exercise in disappointment for all concerned.

Eventually, frustrated teachers and youthworkers realized that it would be more effective to teach to children's strengths and talents, rather than to focus on their deficits. But a large percentage of children who fall through the cracks in school are still characterized as having some learning disability or emotional or behavioral disorder. This places a child at a disadvantage from the very beginning, for school is where early socialization either succeeds or fails. As multitudes of studies have confirmed, when a child feels like a failure, his or her actions soon express and confirm that negative belief.

As a result, by the middle elementary years, kids who don't succeed in school come to believe they are "dumb" and lose motivation to learn. Many of these kids are drawn to other youth who also hate school and teachers. Attached to like-minded peers, they artificially inflate their empty sense of self-worth by rejecting the school that has devalued them.

"When Toby entered middle school and was suddenly required to sit through six or seven lectures a day, he just couldn't do it," explained his mother. "He is a very active, tactile, social learner; all of which his elementary school teachers recognized and were able to accommodate."

"But the cookie-cutter approach to education that he encountered in middle school set him up for almost immediate failure," she continued. "I think that failure caused him to make a subconscious decision in the sixth grade—to write off school. And unfortunately, he never reversed that decision."

Half of students with serious emotional and behavioral problems drop out of school. In fact, they are less likely to graduate than students with mental retardation![2]

Discouraging outcome statistics for conduct-problem youth are often interpreted as evidence that they have lifelong disabilities or are below average in intelligence. But it is the teaching and discipline methods that are backward, not the students, according to many experts.[3] Efforts focused on controlling and training kids for obedience, rather than on stimulating social, emotional, and academic learning, produce kids who are too busy fighting adults to learn from them.

The National Institutes of Health note that fifteen percent of the general population has some learning disability,[4] but up to *fifty* percent of juvenile offenders are labeled as learning disabled.[5] Struggling with traditional learning is a major contributor to delinquent behavior.

Of the nearly four million school-age children who have been deemed to have learning disabilities, at least twenty percent have a disorder that leaves them unable to focus their attention.[6] Some have attention deficit disorders (ADD) and are easily distracted or appear to daydream excessively. In many affected children— mostly boys—the attention deficit is accompanied by hyperactivity (ADHD). Such children act impulsively, blurt out answers, and interrupt. Even when tired, they have trouble sitting still.

Before long, they are in conflict with teachers. Soon new letters are added to their file, such as the ironic acronym ODD (oppositional defiant disorder).

One father said this of his son with ADHD: "In some ways it would have been easier if my boy had a physical disability. Then the school makes ramps, and people cheer whenever small progress is made. But because his disability is not physical, they are only frustrated and fed up with him."

A growing number of educators and researchers are convinced, however, that many children who have been labeled with learning problems and attention disorders are simply children who are not taught in the ways they can learn. For example, in Dr. Thomas Armstrong's book *The Myth of the A.D.D. Child: 50 Ways to Improve Your Child's Behavior and Attention Span Without Drugs, Labels, or Coercion,* he criticizes the currently popular label "attention deficit disorder" as being too simplistic and negative. As an alternative, he provides a wellness perspective with fifty solid strategies to help.[7]

Similarly, Howard Gardner of Harvard University, in *Intelligence Reframed: Multiple Intelligences for the 21st Century,* identifies nine different kinds of intelligence. Each involves different learning approaches.[8] Gardner's nine learning styles are summarized in Figure 1, and there is a reproducible self-assessment in the Appendix on page 139.

Figure 1

Nine Types of Intelligence

1. Linguistic intelligence (word smart)
2. Logical-mathematical intelligence (number smart)
3. Spatial intelligence (image smart)
4. Musical intelligence (music smart)
5. Kinesthetic intelligence (body smart)
6. Interpersonal intelligence (people smart)
7. Intrapersonal intelligence (self smart)
8. Naturalist intelligence (nature smart)
9. Existential intelligence (idea smart)

Very few people are talented in all nine domains. This is probably by design, since a group of individuals with complementary abilities makes a more powerful unit than one in which all have the same strengths and limitations.

But while people have successful careers using each of these learning styles, most schools and aptitude testing focus only on linguistic and logical-mathematical intelligence—a very narrow and exclusionary definition of intelligence. Further, most schools still only celebrate children who perform well in commonly appreciated intelligences (as demonstrated through athletic ability or good grades).

Schools also often promote competition over cooperation: The majority of games and athletics separate kids into "winners" and "losers." Scores of kids whose strengths are not immediately apparent feel left out. Many end up hating school. Some, as we've seen earlier, take the message of "loser" to heart and become reclusive and self-loathing. Others turn to bullying in a misguided attempt to show their strength.

Ultimately, each child has a unique mix of abilities. But regardless of natural variations and limitations in how they learn, all children have strengths and resilience. All children have brains designed to solve problems, in school as in life.

The Power of the Problem-Solving Brain

Psychologists contend that the primary purpose of the logical human brain is solving problems to develop competence.[9] Wrestling with problems is part of the natural process of growth, and doing it successfully is a talent that can be nurtured like any other skill. At-risk children in particular need problem-solving skills in order to level the playing field and allow them to fully develop all of their intelligence. Fourteen-year-old Karl explains: "As you encounter one stressful experience, it strengthens you, like a vaccine, for future crisis. . . . You have to bounce back or you couldn't go on."[10]

In fact, children who are overprotected or "overprivileged" may be ill-equipped to deal with life's inevitable challenges. The difference between those who are seen as "seriously disturbed" and those who are seen as "normal" is not a question of having problems, but of *handling* problems. Those who use faulty coping behavior become more vulnerable, but that can be reversed as they learn more effective coping mechanisms.[11]

The human brain specializes in problem-solving and keeps searching for solutions for any unsolved problems. This is called the Zeigarnik effect.[12] For example, when you can't remember the name of a person you should know, your brain keeps scanning your memory bank, even after you give up trying to retrieve the name. At last the solution pops into your mind, often when you least expect it.

The good news about the Zeigarnik effect is that if someone has not solved a problem, he or she has an inborn motivation to keep trying. The brain wrestles with problems in two ways:

- *Private thought* to reflect and make plans. Most of us solve routine problems this way. If depressed about a serious problem, we may withdraw from others and ruminate and worry.

- *Talking with others* to gain support and a fresh perspective. This is often the best way to solve serious problems, but it requires a safe, trusted confidant. That is where an adult mentor can step in to make a critical difference in a young person's life.

A century ago, John Dewey observed that all problem-solving starts with some "felt difficulty."[13] This applies to academics, sports, hobbies, and any other domain in which youth seek to develop mastery and achieve goals.

The traditional mission of most schools focuses heavily on academics, but also recognizes that optimal development involves a full range of social, emotional, and academic learning.[14] The evidence is clear: Students cannot develop their talents academically or otherwise unless we also address social and emotional growth.

Kids with social and emotional problems often have great gaps in interpersonal problem-solving skills. This has led to a proliferation of social-skills curriculums. Despite initially positive results, the long-term effectiveness of much of this formal training has not been transferable once kids return to their original environment.[15] Skills taught with an artificial curriculum and in an artificial setting do not readily transfer to the natural environment.

Preventive Curriculums

More powerful interventions move problem-solving into the natural life space where kids experience difficulties.[16] In recent years many innovative social-skills and problem-solving curriculums have been designed to use problems or crises for teaching and positive youth development.

The following three model school-based curriculums focus on proactively preparing children with problem-solving skills before serious problems arise.

- *Interpersonal Cognitive Problem Solving (ICPS)* teaches problem-solving skills to young children through a curriculum including activities, puppets, role-playing, and group discussion.[17] When conflicts arise, teachers and parents help children apply their new skills through dialoging about thinking and behavior. Students learn to think for themselves and make good decisions.

- *Promoting Alternative Thinking Strategies (PATHS)* is a violence-prevention program teaching self-control, management of emotions, social problem-solving, and positive peer relations.[18] It is taught by elementary school teachers who enlist other staff and parents to use "teachable moments" to reinforce these skills. This curriculum draws heavily from research on the brain and social and emotional learning.

- *Resolving Conflict Creatively Program (RCCP)* is a K–12 school-wide intervention including training for teachers, administrators, and parents, as well as a curriculum for students.[19] Lessons cover problem-solving, perspective-taking, negotiation, decision-making, and peer mediation. RCCP was piloted in urban settings and seeks to create "peaceable schools" with climates of respect.

Strength-Based Interventions

When problems are already evident, seriously troubled and at-risk youth can benefit from strength-based treatment interventions. Each of the models described below uses behavioral problems as therapeutic teaching opportunities to nurture skills and talents.

- *Positive Peer Culture (PPC)* uses peer-helping groups to reverse negative youth climates that are common in settings serving antisocial youth.[20] Young persons learn to take responsibility for their behavior and exercise positive influence with peers.[21]

- *The EQUIP Program* is an extension of PPC designed to "equip" youth with skills to be more effective peer helpers.[22] Youth receive added training in social skills, anger management, and cognitive moral development. The goal is to develop empathy and responsibility in once antisocial youth.

- *Life Space Crisis Intervention (LSCI)* is a therapeutic method for professionals dealing with youth in crisis.[23] It includes talking strategies to help a youth examine self-defeating thinking, feeling, and behavior and develop prosocial attitudes and skills.

These prevention and treatment programs all focus on building strengths and talents by teaching kids how to replace destructive or self-defeating behavior with new coping strategies. Each has shown positive outcomes with specific populations. Most require significant training and must be implemented across an entire organization for maximum benefit.

The remainder of this chapter will focus on RAP, an innovative intervention based on the Circle of Courage, brain research, and resilience science. Learning how to effectively navigate through problems and conflicts is one of the greatest talents kids can attain for success in life.

RAP: A Strategy for Developing Problem-Solving Skills

Response Ability Pathways, or simply RAP, is a universal intervention that can be used in any setting for children and youth. All who are concerned with young people need the ability to respond to needs, rather than merely react to problems. RAP provides basic training in using natural interactions to develop resilience. Practical, proven strategies guide young persons on the road to responsibility.

RAP uses the normal everyday problems faced by children in home, school, or community as the basis for positive discipline and guidance.[24] If a child exhibits challenging behavior or shows emotional frustration, these natural life events can be used as a curriculum for teaching resilience.

The goal is to strengthen coping skills, self-control, and conscience. RAP is useful for routine problems that all parents experience with their children and is equally applicable in helping troubled youth shift from destructive into constructive behavior.

RAP can take as much time as the teaching moment allows, whether literally a moment or an hour. A series of short RAP interventions distributed over time can sometimes produce more motivation for change than marathon counseling sessions.[25] Nonetheless, RAP is a targeted intervention designed to bring immediate payoffs.

As seen in Figure 2, RAP interventions tap and strengthen three natural abilities related to resilience: *connecting* for support, *clarifying* challenges, and *restoring* harmony.

Figure 2

Response Ability Pathways: The Process and Goals

Connect	Clarify	Restore
• Trust	• Challenge	• Belonging
• Respect	• Logic	• Mastery
• Understanding	• Emotions	• Independence
	• Actions	• Generosity
	• Results	
Strengthen natural ability to build connections and gain positive support	*Strengthen natural ability to clarify challenges and creatively solve problems*	*Strengthen natural ability to restore harmony and take responsible pathways*

Connecting: Listening to Kids' Stories

The first step in RAP, and the foundation for any meaningful interaction with kids, is to connect with them. The biggest challenge to connecting, says counseling professor Jean Peterson, is to stifle our urge to "fix" kids and to learn to simply listen. Noted child psychologist Fritz Redl proposed that to understand children's problems, we should forego fancy diagnosis and simply talk with them about immediate here-and-now events in their life.[26] Of course, listening to such stories does not replace therapy and other interventions for deeply troubled youth. Talking about everyday experience can be therapeutic, but it is not therapy. It is what people do naturally. Even when meeting friends, kids invite stories with the greeting, "What's happening?"

As the chapter on building trust noted, all kids have some story they yearn to tell—if a trusted listener can be found. Adults who have already built a connection to a youth are in the best position to engage in these discussions, and often it's in this very act of listening that the connection actually occurs.

RAP begins with one simple step: Invite a young person to recount a recent event that is significant to him or her. For example, perhaps a youth has just experienced some exciting success, or has been in some trouble at school. Kids are primed to talk about such daily events, and this process of engaging young people in retelling and processing a current story helps them make sense out of those events. It also gives parents and mentors insight into how the youth is thinking and feeling about those events.

The analogy of an iceberg can be helpful here (see Figure 3). The outward, exposed behavior (the "outside" kid) represents only 10 percent of the whole story. The other 90 percent of the story remains hidden in the "inside" kid. There lie the thinking patterns and emotions that have greatly contributed to a young person's behavior—behavior that actually makes sense if the observer can understand what's going on under the surface. Engaging a young person in telling his or her story from a curious, investigative, nonjudgmental place allows the youth and the adult to lower the water level on the iceberg and take a more extended look below.

Figure 3

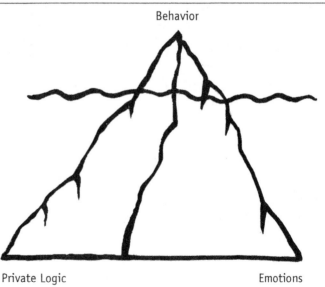

Behavior

Private Logic   Emotions

The advantage of exploring life events in this way is that almost anybody can understand them. Parents, mentors, and young people can all make sense of verbal accounts of events. And as we have seen in our discussion of the brain, verbalizing experiences helps tame the limbic brain's confusing raw emotion into material that young people can communicate to others, examine, and learn from.

Discussing current events keeps the focus on manageable issues and feelings. We are not digging into deep problems of the distant past, although they inevitably come up when someone is struggling to process a current situation. And people are naturally inclined to share those unresolved problems with trusted friends or mentors.[27] Our intent, however, is not to force youth to disclose painful material they may not wish to reveal or reopen past wounds. Rather, we are helping youth explore practical questions: "How is my behavior helping or hindering me from achieving my goals?" "How does my behavior affect others?"

Effective mentors avoid intrusive questions. Instead, they find opportunities to follow up on what a youth says. They listen carefully for "window words," which offer an opening for expressing interest or asking questions. In the following exchange, notice how the mentor waits for the youth to bring up what is bothering her, and then responds out of a natural, caring stance:

Mentor: Hi, Tricia. How are you doing?

Tricia: Terrible. My mother told me I had to talk with you about my problem.

Mentor: What problem is that?

Tricia: I don't want to talk about it.

Mentor: Okay. No problem. Would you like me to grab a soda for you?

While Tricia initially expresses unwillingness to discuss her problem, the mentor takes her very presence and the fact that she brought it up as a positive indicator and an actual bid for more discussion. She gets Tricia a soda to give her a little time to think and to help her feel settled and ready to talk for a while if she so chooses.

Tricia: I hate it when my mom gets all worked up about every little thing.

Mentor: What is it that she's worked up about?

Tricia: I went to a party, and she thinks I have a big drinking problem.

Mentor: So what do you think?

Tricia: I don't think I have a problem. I only had three beers. Everybody else was getting wasted. I was practically the only one who kept my head together.

Mentor: So you don't see any grounds to your mother's concerns?

Tricia: Not really. But, yeah, in some ways I can see where maybe I have somewhat of a drinking problem. But just yelling at me is only going to make things worse. In some ways, getting in trouble is about the only way we can even have conversations. Otherwise she's too busy to even talk to me.

As Tricia shares details about the event, the mentor listens. In time Tricia drops her defensiveness and comes to the conclusion that she made a very unwise choice in attending the party. She also decides to tell her Mom the full story of what happened to repair their strained relationship.

Mentor: What do you think would make things better?

Tricia: Just talking about it. And probably going to that group I used to go last year, after my dad left.

Mentor: So what would you like to do about all of this?

Tricia: I think I should start by talking to my mom. Maybe if I admit my stuff first, she'll admit her own stuff, too, and then we can talk for real.

Mentor: That sounds like a really good idea. Would you like me to be there when you talk to your mom today, or do you want to do it alone?

Tricia: You mean talk to her now?

Mentor: It seems like it's a pretty important issue to both of you. Do you see any reason not to talk about it now?

Tricia: Well—it's just hard. Maybe it would be good if you were there.

Mentor: I would be happy to be there.

For youth to make significant strides in changing their behavior, they must begin by honestly examining how they think, feel, and experience the world. Over time, as a young person discusses various life events, if an adult listens carefully and responds with respect, a relationship of trust develops. An attentive listener will see recurring destructive patterns in the young person's approach to problems. Then the adult can nurture the youth's most basic talent: the ability to recognize and change those patterns.

It's also important to recognize that there are two conversations going on in every interchange: what you are saying, and what the other person is saying to him- or herself *about* what you're saying. The latter conversation has the most influence on the listener's response. Father Anthony De Mello, from India, said it another way: "You see persons and things not as they are, but as *you* are."[28] This is true for youth and adults. So listening intently to how someone is *interpreting* an event tells you much more about that individual than simply getting to the bottom of what "really" happened.

Clarifying: Tracking CLEAR Thinking

The source of destructive behavior patterns lies in destructive *thinking* patterns. John Gibbs has simplified a mass of research on cognitive psychology into common thinking errors that underlie most problem behavior: blaming, assuming the worst, minimizing and mislabeling, and self-centered thinking.[29] These can be remembered by the letters BAMMS.

- Blaming—not taking responsibility or wallowing in self-blame.

  That teacher just hates me.

- Assuming the worst—taking a pessimistic approach or believing that others have hostile intentions.

  Adults always lie to me.

- Minimizing and mislabeling—describing harmful behavior as if it is okay; belittling others.

  So I hit him. He's a wuss.

- Self-centered thinking—dwelling on one's own needs and being inconsiderate of others.

  If I want something, I take it.

To some degree, all of us can be tricked by distorted thinking. Because the source of most thinking errors is a preoccupation with one's own needs, desires, and feelings, the solution is to clarify thinking. Clear thinking reflects "the big picture" outside the confines of private logic. And once we can see the situation from outside our own perspective, we can develop empathy for others.

Establishing a CLEAR Timeline. It helps to construct a timeline of events as we listen to kids' stories of life events and try to help them make sense out of the challenges they face. We want to understand not just what kids do, but why, and how they feel about what's happened. This requires listening carefully to the young person in question, as he or she is the only one who knows what is really going on with the inside kid. Figure 4 shows the pathway triggered by a stressful event.

Figure 4

93

CLEAR Timeline

| Challenge | Logic | Emotions | Actions | Results |

The acronym CLEAR describes a listening roadmap to help get below the surface of the iceberg and uncover destructive thinking errors. As we listen to a child talking about an event, we should ask ourselves the corresponding questions for each stage.

- *Challenge* is posed by external or internal events that create stress or "felt difficulty": What triggered the conflict?

- *Logic* refers to inner perceptions and thoughts: What was the child thinking as events unfolded?

- *Emotions* propel a person toward some preprogrammed course of action: What specific feelings motivated the child's behavior?

- *Actions* are behaviors directed to achieve some goal: What was the purpose of the child's coping behavior?

- *Results* are consequences of actions: What was the outcome in the reactions of others and in achieving the child's goals?

Of course, you can't just lay this list out for kids—you need to quietly listen first—though sometimes it's helpful later to work through and write out the timeline with the young person. It's also not necessarily a sequential, linear process (hence the arrow in Figure 4 points both ways). You can go back and forth, but these are the important components to keep in the back of your mind.

Restoring: Bringing Resolution and Building Strengths

The final stage in RAP is to restore what may have been broken during the conflict or situation that the youth is recounting with you. Restoring harmony does not require permanent solutions to every one of a kid's problems. Rome was not built in a day. At the same time, restoring doesn't necessarily require a long, drawn-out session. If you can nurture one strength or talent—if you can show a youth how to repair one broken bond—you are setting him or her on the road to resilience, one step at a time.

A RAP in Action

Some aberrant behavior is just acting up—normal exaggerated teenage reactions like moaning and groaning about chores or staying out fifteen minutes past curfew—and requires a relatively brief interaction to get the youth back on a more positive track.

Other times, behavior is acting *out* and stems from some problem other than the obvious issue at hand. When a youth reacts to ordinary situations—a request to babysit a sibling or a question about an overdue assignment—with emotions stronger than annoyance, he or she may be transferring unresolved anger from a previous context. Something in the interaction, even just a tone or a facial expression, may have triggered a traumatic memory and signaled threat or danger, even though the current context is not dangerous at all.

Effective use of the RAP strategy, as the following example shows, can uncover some of these root causes as well as help youth to gain more control over their consequences.

A girl known by peers as "Wild Wilma" is kicked out of class and sent to you, the school guidance counselor. You've been told she's a troublemaker, but you can't see how that label helps. After all, a doctor would never call a patient an "illnessmaker." Youth in conflict are trying to cope in ways that make sense to them, even if it makes no sense to others.

Instead of jumping to conclusions or reverting to automatic responses, you decide to find time to talk to Wilma in order to better understand what happened. You don't presume her initial answer will be a clear statement of events. "The teacher is a jerk" is more her style. But you know that unless she can learn to think more clearly about how her behavior affects others, she is likely to keep making serious mistakes.

You've seen how kids like Wilma continually find themselves caught up in self-defeating patterns of behavior or conflict cycles.[30] For some reason, Wilma keeps making things worse for herself and doesn't seem to learn from punishment. You wonder if teachers, administrators, and others in authority have been asking the wrong question: Rather than, "What kind of consequence can I administer to change Wilma's behavior?" you wonder if they should be asking, "Why does Wilma's behavior persist, despite punitive consequences?"

You don't want to make the same old mistakes in problem-solving by blaming Wilma or assuming the worst about her. Instead, you give Wilma the benefit of the doubt. You assume she probably has reasons for her behavior, and you hope to learn more about the private logic that keeps leading her toward bad choices. Maybe, you think, you can help her see herself and her world in a different light.

Wilma needs to learn new strategies. Of course, people have been trying to tell her this for some time, but she refuses to listen. How has she become so convinced that everybody is against her, and that she has to keep fighting adults?

When facing stress or challenge, everyone has a standard system for coping. To help understand what causes Wilma to become "wild," you decide you will track the CLEAR timeline of her coping cycle, asking yourself the appropriate questions as she tells her side of the story:

- *Challenge:* What was the trigger that set Wilma off?
- *Logic:* What was Wilma thinking as this event escalated?
- *Emotions:* What specific feelings motivated Wilma's behavior?
- *Actions:* What was the purpose of Wilma's coping behavior?
- *Results:* What was the outcome of Wilma's behavior, and what were the reactions of others?

Before you can help Wilma think clearly, she has to calm down. If she is swearing, slamming her books down, and insulting the school secretary, she is in no position to begin rational problem-solving.

You know just yelling "Calm down!" will probably make Wild Wilma even wilder. You must form some connection to her so that she doesn't see you as the enemy. Only then will she be willing to share what happened from her point of view. Maybe if you listen, she will listen as well.

Connecting for support. You find a place to talk where Wilma won't have to perform for peers. She initially refuses to sit down, but you don't make a big deal of it. She vents her anger at you and says this school sucks and all the staff are . . . whatever. . . . You repeat to yourself three times, *I am a thermostat, not a thermometer.*

You don't tell her she shouldn't feel this way, because she no doubt has her reasons. Since you are doing nothing to stir it, her fury begins to subside. She angrily plops into the chair. "This has been a hard day for you," you say in a kind voice. Amazingly, she starts to cry.

You hand her a box of tissues. *She will probably refuse my bid for connection,* you think, but she takes the box and says, "Thanks." So far, so good. She is calming down, and your tone of voice keeps her from mixing you up with Mr. Jerk or whatever her name for him might be.

Clarifying the problem. Wilma waits for you to make the next move. "Can you help me understand what happened back there?" you ask, in the least blaming tone you can pull off. Slowly, the two of you sort out the timeline of events.

As it turns out, this was actually one of her better teachers, but Wilma was having a lousy day. She had a huge blow up last night with her mother's boyfriend and, no, she doesn't want to talk about it right now.

In any case, Mr. J. corrected Wilma for talking with her friends, which seemed to be the "challenge" that triggered her anger. He reacted with a flash of irritation, and this was all the stress it took to set her off. She and the teacher traded tit-for-tat barbs and the next thing she knew, today was looking a lot like last night.

Caught up in an angry struggle, Wilma was thinking, *He treats me like crap, and I don't have to take it any more.* She became more and more incensed, and when she muttered a profanity, she was sent out of class. She didn't want to get kicked out, but, hey, she had her payoff. She showed folks she wouldn't take garbage from anybody.

By now, the RAP has taken twenty minutes, and classes will soon be switching. It's time for some resolution.

Restoring harmony. "I really appreciate your maturity in helping sort out this problem, Wilma," you say. "Do you have any thoughts about what you want to do as a result of our conversation?"

"Yup," she answers. "Next time I need to think before I spout off."

Mirroring her idea back to her, you say: "Yup, don't just do something, stand there!" Wilma groans at your attempt at humor, but laughs a little, too. She gets the point, and in the process you've given her some mastery in developing a new coping talent: You've nurtured her ability to avoid conflict. In the future, you hope, Wilma can stay in class (and build her academic talents).

"Another thing," she volunteers, "maybe I should apologize, but he's probably still mad at me." You offer to come along to check with the teacher. The timing is right, since classes are changing. And a broken bond is repaired as a result. The reconciliation takes but thirty seconds and goes pretty well. Wilma seems genuine, and the teacher doesn't appear to hold a grudge.

Now that the fight is gone, Wilma seems like a scared little girl. You know this is not the end of her problems, but you hope that next time it will be easier for her to talk about what's bothering her, rather than to explode. You invite her to stop by and chat again, and she says, "Thanks."

After Wilma leaves, you remember that you wanted to take time to draw out the timeline for her on a piece of paper. You could have helped her see events more clearly: She started the day on edge, then a minor stressful event triggered angry thoughts and emotions. She reacted instead of thinking clearly and was booted from class. Knowing Wilma, you guess you might have another chance to talk.

Reaching the Inside Kid

Reading this account of a RAP makes it look easy. But there are many things happening beneath the surface that contribute to the success of this kind of interaction.

The ability of the adult to form a positive connection is crucial. Adult-wary kids are masters at seeing through our words to what's really in our hearts. When bids for connection convey genuine concern and empathy, kids eventually invite us to connect. But when kid-wary adults react to provocative behavior, young people quickly shut down or detach.

Troubled kids are often like the director of a play, casting others to act out their own emotions. Often, after an encounter with a raging teen, adults find themselves filled with anger, even though they were calm just moments before. Similarly, sometimes talking with a depressed young person leaves the adult feeling down and blue.

We naturally empathize with the feelings of others. It's what allows us to connect. In fact, as we listen to a young person's painful story, we can use our own feelings as a gauge of how that kid feels telling—and living out—the story. But having feelings doesn't mean we have to act on them. Repressing that urge to act on feelings requires that we gain some altitude over the situation, rather than being submerged under it.[31]

Showing support and empathy, regardless of how we might initially feel, is essential if we are to avoid being cast in the role of enemy. We must also recognize that the angry encounters we experience with youth are not primarily about us. There are many other things going on in the lives of troubled children, and sometimes, as teachers and caregivers, we experience the brunt of their rage simply because we are the safest target for their anger.

At the same time, it is important not to downplay young people's feelings, not to try to convince them they shouldn't feel the way they do. In fact, kids who are very upset will generally feel disconnected from an adult who is deadpan calm and doesn't seem to notice the intensity of their concerns.

And so to some extent, we need to mirror the degree of a child's feelings, just as a parent would. If the child feels distressed, we should show empathy and genuine concern. If the child feels positive, we should share his or her happiness.[32]

It is also important to realize that effective intervention is a process. It doesn't happen all at once, and it especially doesn't happen in the heat of a crisis. When someone feels extreme fear or anger, the brain's centers for rational thinking and positive emotions shut down. A young person who is operating in survival mode is not ready to solve problems. Sometimes leaving a very distressed person to cool off in isolation works, but at other times that only fuels anger and alienation. Often, in times of crisis, what's most effective is just *being together* with the young person. As we walk through the storm with him or her, we form a strong connection. As RAP and other strength-based problem-solving models illustrate, entering into a young person's conflict as a *partner* with him or her can offer one of the most powerful models for building problem-solving skills.

Nurturing talent in its most obvious form encompasses recognizing and cultivating the many different types of intelligence present in each of us. We tend to confuse intelligence with academic success, but conflicts with teachers, parents, and other students can derail troubled kids, kids who may already be struggling with learning disabilities and a sense of failure. If we remember that challenging kids are more likely to struggle academically— at least with the linguistic and mathematical intelligence on which most traditional education focuses—we can understand their frustration and acting out in class much more. And, hopefully, we can offer alternative teaching styles that are better suited for the other seven learning intelligences.

Nurturing talent, then, means more than signing a kid up for a math study group or for guitar lessons, though those things are important, too; nurturing talent also means fostering critical problem-solving skills necessary for healthy development into adulthood, as those are the essential foundation for developing all other talents.

We conclude this chapter with some practical tips (Figure 5) on how to effectively listen to and nurture talent in young people who are challenging.

Figure 5

Tips for Nurturing Talent[33]

1. **Give your full attention.** Show genuine interest and respect. Give affirmation and validation. Never act bored or distracted.
   I'm glad you stopped by. Let me turn off my cell phone and put this work away. What's on your mind?
2. **Ask to learn more.** Use "window words" from the conversation to follow up and get more information.
   You mentioned "lots of interests." What is most exciting to you right now?
3. **Match their tempo.** Don't rush or be afraid of silences that can be time for reflection. Don't control with irrelevant or probing interrogation.
   Take your time. I'm listening.
4. **Paraphrase what they say.** Make sure they know you are trying to understand.
   Sounds like you thought nobody was interested in your ideas.
5. **Reflect back their feelings.** Express empathy to convey your support and concern.
   That must have been really difficult for you.
6. **Encourage full expression.** Use open-ended questions instead of yes-or-no questions. Avoid "why" questions that trigger defensiveness. Show interest and curiosity.
   Can you help me understand what you wanted to happen?
7. **Avoid blaming.** Don't correct or blame. Don't preach about what someone should or shouldn't do.
   How did you feel after that fight with your mom?
8. **Avoid detracting comments.** Don't dismiss or minimize their problems. Don't say you know "exactly" how someone else feels.
   So it sounds like how you dress is an important form of self-expression for you.
9. **Respect personal space.** Don't force intimacy. Offer a blend of empathy and objectivity.
   It must be hard to have an earlier curfew than your friends. What do you think your mom is worried about when you're out late?
10. **Celebrate survivor's pride.** Validate acts of strength and resilience.
    You showed real courage in facing and working on that problem.

Endnotes

[1] S. D. Brooks was superintendent of a New York training school in the mid-19th century.

[2] Wagner 1995, 99.

[3] Cambone 1994.

[4] Ross-Kidder 2002.

[5] LD Online n.d.

[6] Neuwirth 1993.

[7] Armstrong 1997.

[8] Gardner 2000.

[9] White 1959.

[10] Murphy and Moriarity 1976, 263.

[11] Murphy and Moriarity 1976.

[12] Bluma Zeigarnik, a Russian psychologist, first discovered this phenomenon in 1927.

[13] Dewey [1910] 1960, 72.

[14] Zins 2004.

[15] Mathur and Rutherford 1996.

[16] Goldstein and Martens 2000.

[17] Shure 1992.

[18] Kusche and Greenberg 1994.

[19] Lantieri and Patti 1996.

[20] Vorrath and Brendtro 1985.

[21] Gold and Osgood 1992.

[22] Gibbs, Potter, and Goldstein 1995.

[23] Long, Wood, and Fecser 2001.

[24] Hoffman 2002.

[25] Miller and Rollnick 1991.

[26] Redl 1994.

[27] Pennebaker 1990.

[28] De Mello 1992, 47.

[29] Gibbs, Potter, and Goldstein 1995.

[30] These have been called conflict cycles (Long and Dufner 1980); stress cycles (Flach 1989); angry escalation (Zillman 1993); argument cycles (Scheff 1995); recidivism cycles (Toch and Adams, 2002); and coercive cycles (Patterson 2002a).

[31] Taken from Nick Long's comments at a teleconference training in Washington, DC for Children and Family Bureau–funded youth shelters in January 2003.

[32] Clarke 1999.

[33] Adapted from J. S. Peterson 2003. The term "survivor's pride" was coined by psychiatrist Steve Wolin.

chapter five

Promoting Power

Our worst fear is not that we are inadequate. Our deepest fear is that we are powerful beyond measure. It is our light, not our darkness, that most frightens us.

—Nelson Mandela[1]

Jason had been locked up for four years before transitioning into one of Straight Ahead Ministries' aftercare homes. His first couple of months went pretty smoothly. But one night, after going out with some friends, he came home very drunk.

Since he seemed unable to handle the amount of freedom and responsibility he had been given, Jason was restricted to the house for a couple of weeks, except when he was at work, school, or an approved activity. During that period we observed that he was particularly difficult to wake up for school. He was always tired. That didn't make any sense to us, since he was at home now more than ever.

One day, after Jason's grounding was over, he said to us, "You probably noticed how tired I was during the past few weeks." We said we had certainly noticed and asked why that was so. "Believe it or not," Jason said, "I would get up at one or two o'clock in the morning, when everyone else was sleeping, and walk around outside."

"So what were you doing?" we asked. "Hooking up with your old friends? Drinking by yourself?"

He shrugged. "I wasn't doing anything. I was just walking."

Prior to the grounding, Jason had never gone on midnight strolls, nor did he take them after those few weeks of grounding were over. When asked why he'd risked further punishment for something that didn't seem to serve any purpose, he said, "I guess just because you told me I couldn't."

We adults tend to define success with kids as getting them to do what we think is "right." But as Jason's story illustrates, teens tend to define success for themselves as exercising independence. Helping kids understand the connection between independence and responsibility is a necessary component in empowering them to take ownership for their choices.

Most of us feel that responsibility is very critical for young people to develop. But as educator W. E. B. Du Bois said, "Responsibility is the first step in responsibility."[2] One survey revealed that teens feel they have a voice in what they do only twenty percent of the time. Only responsibility teaches responsibility. Fostering responsibility in youth requires granting power to them, even though that process can be quite threatening for those in authority.

Authentic power does involve responsibility. Kids may not recognize how much power they already possess, however, so they often buy into the notion that adults can control their lives. When kids can see that it is they and they alone who possess the ultimate power over how they choose to live their lives, they can begin to exercise that power to their benefit, instead of their detriment. The key to teaching responsibility lies in promoting kids' autonomy and personal power, rather than demanding mere obedience. Once kids feel empowered, they will rise to the challenge of taking on more responsibility.

Landmarks of Responsibility

Powerless persons can never exercise responsibility. Young people who don't feel in charge of their destiny have no destiny, but are tossed like a rudderless boat on a stormy sea, buffeted by life's difficulties. They are unsure of their own worth. They may act in ways that cause harm to self, or turn their pain outward and hurt others. But as they take responsibility for their behavior, they can begin to change the direction of their lives.

The chart on page 106 (Figure 1) describes landmarks for youth in pain on the road to resilience. Three major dimensions of problem behavior are listed in the left column: feelings of poor self-worth, disrespect for self, and disrespect for others.[3] The left column describes weakness. The right column illustrates the power youth experience as they learn to overcome these problems. In short:

- Youth who felt unworthy come to see they are persons of value.

- Youth who acted with disrespect to self develop new self-respect.

- Youth who have hurt others learn to treat others with respect.

People will do many harmful things in an attempt to gain or retain power. Whenever someone conceives power as just the application of force to get one's own way, great damage results—whether the person abusing power is a bullying youth or a dictatorial adult. That definition of power infers the need to control others, to be right, or to enjoy unearned privilege.

Figure 1

Landmarks of Responsibility

Pain-Based Problems

Poor Self-Worth
Has a low opinion of self. Feels put down and mistreated. Worries about what is wrong with self. Expects rejection or hostility and is afraid to trust others. Can't face others with confidence, but feels self-conscious or puts up a front. Is insecure with persons of higher rank. Does not feel good enough to be accepted by positive persons.

Disrespects Self
Acts in ways that hurt self. Puts self down, provoking ridicule, punishment, or rejection. Doesn't try to solve problems or improve self. Feels hopeless or blames others. Allows others to mislead or inflict harm. Acts without concern for the future. Intentionally engages in risky or self-destructive behaviors. Doesn't learn from mistakes, but repeats self-defeating behaviors.

Disrespects Others
Acts in ways that hurt others. Is selfish, doesn't care about the needs or feelings of others. Seeks to build self up by using or abusing others. Enjoys putting people down and doesn't show concern for others. Bullies or takes advantage of weaker persons and those with problems. Seldom helps others, except perhaps family members or those in a small circle of so-called friends.

Resilient Achievements

Strong Self-Worth
Has realistic self-confidence. Does not see self as a victim. Doesn't feel sorry for self, but recognizes strengths and accepts shortcomings. Cannot easily be made to feel small or inferior and builds trust with caring persons. Does not need to puff up self or hide behind a false front. Can be appropriately assertive to those in power. Feels good enough to be accepted by anybody.

Respects Self
Values self. Doesn't put self down. Takes responsibility for actions and works to improve self. Tries to solve problems and doesn't give up easily or blame others. Distances self from persons or situations that are destructive. Thinks ahead, is hopeful about the future, and sets goals for self. Does not purposely do things likely to hurt self. Is not afraid to ask for help. Uses problems as learning opportunities.

Respects Others
Values others. Seeks to help others. Shows concern, even if persons are not liked or well-known. Values the opinions and feelings of others and treats them fairly. Does not participate in ridicule or bullying. Makes an effort to stand up for those who are hurt or friendless and support them in facing difficulties. Is generous and shows respect to all persons, recognizing that every person deserves to be treated with dignity.

Differentiating Rank From Rankism

In *Somebodies and Nobodies* (2004), Robert Fuller terms the abuse of power as "rankism." Whether based on race, sex, age, class, ethnicity, looks, or any other surface distinction, all discrimination has this in common: Persons of lesser rank, the nobodies, are bullied by those in power, the somebodies.

Examples of rankism abound. A boss harassing an employee, a customer barking at a clerk, a coach bullying a player, a principal insulting a teacher, a teacher humiliating a student, students ostracizing weaker peers, a parent belittling a child. Most of us have been both victims and perpetrators of rankism. Rankism is just another form of coercion and bullying.

A teacher recalls distant memories of a fellow seventh-grade nobody who was treated as an outcast by the more popular students:

> I remember there was a school talent show. Tim, a fellow outcast, somehow gathered the courage to sing "The House of the Rising Sun." He'd probably imagined this moment over and over—it was his chance to be somebody.
>
> Well, as soon as he got up on stage and started singing, the catcalls started. He could barely finish his song. You'd think that after being the target of similar abuse, I might have stood up for him, or at least stayed quiet. But instead I joined in the jeering: "Yeah, that Tim is such a jerk." I felt so relieved that for once the target wasn't me.[4]

While rankism is a problem, rank is not. We don't want to level out differences in ability, for we need the most talented doctors, lawyers, soldiers, accountants, pilots, and politicians. In school, we want excellence in teachers and administrators, and also in our athletes, cheerleaders, and scholars.

Striving for rank is a way of expressing competence and our individual talents. Problems only arise when rank becomes an excuse to abuse, humiliate, or subjugate others. When certain ranks are perceived as superior, populations are polarized into the popular and the unpopular, upper class and lower class, the "in" group and the "out" group, the haves and have-nots.

In a respectful school climate, the central ethos is that all people, youth and elders alike, use their power to serve and protect, never to tyrannize or domineer. When persons abuse rank, we don't remain silent or turn away. But even abusers must be confronted with deep respect for their dignity. Confrontation rooted in animosity never succeeds. We should never overcome rankism with more rankism.

This does not mean reckless reforms to eliminate rank, lowering standards, and letting kids run the school. What students want is not to rule, but to be recognized—to be treated as a somebody. One middle school boy put it this way: "All I want is some kind of *noticement*." When all are treated with respect, namely by the Golden Rule, then the terms "somebody" and "nobody" lose their power.

Rather than viewing power as the application of force, or something bestowed upon us through position or title, we offer this alternative definition: *Power is realized through taking responsibility for one's actions and empowering others.*

Redefining Responsibility

When kids and adults hear "responsibility," they tend to migrate in their thinking toward either "blame" or "obligation." While those definitions of responsibility are common in contemporary culture, both completely miss the true meaning of responsibility. True responsibility leads to empowerment and resilience.

- When responsibility is defined as *blame*, it focuses on undesirable past events. When we say, "You're responsible for this problem," we imply that someone deserves punishment. Blame produces feelings of shame if we have done wrong, or feelings of resentment if another has wronged us.

- When responsibility is defined as *obligation*, it focuses on future events. When we say, "You'll be responsible for making sure this problem doesn't happen again," we imply that someone is expected to control an outcome. A sense of

obligation is a burden to anyone, but especially to a youth
already carrying the weight of previous failures to meet
others' expectations.[5]

If responsibility connotes only blame or obligation, it is no surprise that many people would try to avoid it at any cost. But real
responsibility dwells not in the past or future, but in the here
and now. Genuine responsibility empowers, rather than blames
or burdens. Responsibility is not a duty, but an entirely voluntary
act.

As the word itself connotes, "response-ability" involves the ability
to respond to the needs of ourselves and others in the present
moment. Taking charge of our thoughts, feelings, actions, and
resulting consequences fosters responsibility. We abandon the
victim stances of blame and shame; we embrace self-respect, personal power, and a sense of freedom. In short, the end result of
responsibility is a sense of personal power.[6]

Strategies for Developing Responsibility

Kids need to be encouraged for even fledgling attempts at
responsible action. Our natural tendency when dealing with
troubling teens is to revert to deficit-based thinking, to focus all
of our energy on their problems. Unfortunately, most kids are
only recognized when they make poor choices, and their many
positive choices, like doing homework, are ignored. As one youth
told us, "It seems the only time anybody ever pays any attention
to me is when I get into trouble." Another boy in detention said,
"I'd rather be wanted for murder than not wanted at all."

Some adults fear that highlighting good qualities might somehow
send kids the signal that we condone their negative behavior. But
responsibility will never grow in kids when we communicate
that we think of them as untrustworthy or incompetent. We want
to develop trust, to nurture talent, and to create personal power,
not undermine it. A rule of thumb shared by a colleague at Girls
and Boys Town is to give kids ten positive statements about
themselves for every negative one. Our colleague J. C. Chambers
says it another way: "Glance at weaknesses, gaze at strengths."

This demands a great deal of creativity with kids who seem to mask their virtues. But it is the child who is hardest to affirm who needs it most. Kids' latent potentials will not surface automatically. Specific techniques are required to develop positive relationships and group climates that foster responsibility. Here we will highlight several methods that have been developed in programs that are successful with challenging youth.

Define Limits, Choices, and Natural Consequences[7]

In the earlier scenario, Jason saw his only opportunity for independence and success as going against what he perceived that adults had determined for him. Kids are much more powerful when they learn to make good choices from a number of options within defined limits, and when they realize that they have been responsible in the process. Of course, this also means experiencing the natural consequences of their poor choices (see Figure 2).

Figure 2

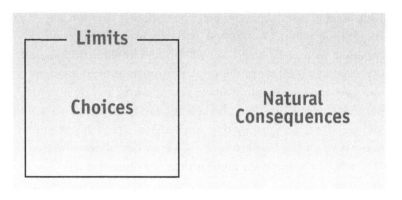

It is the role of responsible adults to set appropriate limits for kids. Without limits, life becomes destabilizing and chaotic, as youth become confused about what is expected of them. One girl told us, "I just wish someone would have cared enough about me to tell me 'No.'"

It's also important to give young people the opportunity to practice making choices within those limits at every age. For example, a father can ask his three-year-old daughter, "Do you want to wear your blue dress or your green jumper today?" Small occasions give kids healthy practice in decision-making. Remember that by definition, a decision offers a choice only if you don't particularly care which option the child chooses. Asking a teenager if he wants to do his homework before or after dinner is giving him a choice; saying, "Either you do your homework, or you're grounded," is a threat.

Of course, kids don't always make healthy choices, and they step outside the established limits. In those cases, using natural consequences is a far more effective tool of preparing them for the real world than doling out unrelated punishments, as most programs serving troubled kids do: Getting detention for not completing your homework offers far less learning than missing out on a fun field trip when the class moves on to the next chapter without you. A good litmus test to distinguish consequences from punishment is to make sure that when the child asks, "Who's making me hurt like this?" he or she has to turn around and say, "Oh, me."[8]

Raising responsible young people is a careful balancing act. We need to keep enough structure to anchor and guide behavior. On the other hand, youth need increasing opportunities to operate on their own by making decisions, failing at times, and gaining confidence.

Sometimes we also need to show young people how they *already* have the power of choice. For example, when Jeffrey says, "The teacher is making me do this homework," he's making a victim statement that infers he has no choice. In actuality, Jeffrey doesn't *have* to do his homework; many other students don't, as frustrated teachers will attest! To transform Jeffrey's sense of being a victim of cruel teachers into a sense of being a powerful agent in his own life, we need to help him see that doing his homework is a choice he is wisely making, rather than something he has to do begrudgingly.

> Mentor: So, what would happen if you chose not to do your homework?
>
> *Jeffrey [shrugs]: I'd fail the assignment.*

Mentor: And what would the consequences of that be?

Jeffrey: I'd probably flunk the class.

Mentor: And what would happen if you flunked the class?

Jeffrey: Then I wouldn't graduate.

Mentor: And what if you didn't graduate?

Jeffrey [sighs dramatically]: I couldn't get a decent job.

Mentor [grins]: And what if you couldn't get a decent job?

Jeffrey: Then, I'd probably end up having to steal to get food.

Mentor: And what if you stole to get food?

Jeffrey: I'd get caught and thrown in jail. [Rolls eyes.] Okay, okay, I get it!

This kind of questioning can go on until the scenario ends in prison, homelessness, or death. It's an exaggerated progression, but the young person gets the point. It is not that he or she *has* to do homework, babysit a sibling, or take out the trash. He or she *chooses* to do those things, because they are the best options. And that is a very empowering realization about an act of genuine responsibility—an act kids already perform all the time without realizing it.

Reverse Responsibility[9]

Until youth learn to assume responsibility for their own behavior and act responsibly towards one another, they have not made lasting change. The most formidable barrier to building responsibility is the youth's private logic of thinking like a victim. This posture either fuels helplessness ("Poor me") or justifies blaming others ("It's not my fault"). Many youngsters have made a fine art out of shifting responsibility to others.

Since youth are skilled at dodging responsibility, adults must be *more* skillful at respectfully *requiring* responsibility. This can be done by simply returning the serve, as in a tennis match. When a youth attempts to shift responsibility by sending it into your court, you lob it back, returning the responsibility to the young person.

These verbal exchanges can become powerful, brief teaching moments for responsibility. The goal is to extricate youth from victim postures by assuming they have the strength to restore relationships. In a responsible posture, a young person can learn from mistakes and move forward, rather than getting mired in blame or cowering in shame.

Below is an example of how to respond to a youth who acts like a helpless pawn of life events:

> *Youth puts off responsibility: Why should I care?*
> *Nobody cares about me.*
>
> Adult reverses responsibility: Then perhaps it's up to you to care about yourself.

Most adults would be tempted to say something like, "But I care." But people who act powerless in the face of problems do not need adults who only feel sorry for them; they need to learn self-efficacy. Tone is crucial is these kinds of conversations. One must speak frankly, but with great concern and empathy. We show how deeply we care by tenaciously conveying our belief that the young person has the positive strength to act in a mature, responsible manner.

Not all irresponsible kids wail in helplessness; others flail at external events or blame others to shift the focus from their own issues. The following example involves comments made in a group discussion, which permitted the adult to model the reversal of responsibility to the entire group:

> *Youth puts off responsibility: What do you expect?*
> *My parents are both drunks.*
>
> Adult reverses responsibility: Is Tony trying to tell the group that everybody with alcoholic parents decides to abuse alcohol?

Reversing responsibility can also be used to get members of a group to embrace their responsibility for helping a troubled peer. In negative cultures, youth feel little obligation to one another. They avoid or attack peers who show problems, or perhaps even encourage problems by laughing at antisocial behavior, a process that is known as deviance coaching.

> *Youth shifts responsibility: John is such a jerk. He always insults everybody. We should give him what he deserves.*

> Adult reverses responsibility: John must be really hurting to act like that. This group is strong enough to help John with his problems instead of getting sucked into his immature behavior by trading insults.

As adults effectively model reversing responsibility, youth themselves will begin to use this style of communication with their friends. One student in a peer-helping program described this technique to a newcomer to the group: "It's like we hold up a mirror, and whatever the problem is, you begin to see it pretty clearly in yourself—as well as the solution!"

Reinterpret the Story

There are many things that happen to us that we cannot control, but we can control how we interpret and respond to what happens to us. Nothing helps shed the victim mentality prevalent in many troubled kids more than grasping this truth: Private logic is not the only logic. Every story and event from our lives can be read from multiple perspectives. Each new angle offers insight, but some perspectives are more helpful than others in creating a positive future. Learning to see those other perspectives is a kind of talent that we can nurture; acting on our new interpretations is a kind of power.

When we interpret our stories with ourselves as powerful agents within them, we are better able to accept responsibility in the most liberating sense of the word. Consider the following scenario.

Mentor: So, Ronald, how did you end up suspended from school?

Youth: My principal.

Mentor: You had nothing to do with it?

Youth: Not really. He just has it in for me, and there's nothing I can do to change that.

As long as the youth refuses to own his own behavior, he remains bitter, powerless, and hopeless about any possible change for the future. But as we dialogue about who is in control of his life, the lights slowly begin to come on.

Mentor: So are you saying that you have no power in this situation? That the principal is the one who controls you?

Youth: Nah. He doesn't control me. I control myself.

Mentor: Okay . . .

Youth: Well—actually—I guess it was me who got myself booted out.

Once Ronald accepts his power to get himself "booted out," he also realizes his power to keep himself *in* school. He can take an active role in his own life for better or for worse, as he chooses, but a passive role will always leave him at the mercy of the world. In that sense, accepting responsibility for his past actions could give him the response-ability to change his future. With that shift in interpretation, Ronald can develop a sense of hope and empowerment over his future.

One of the best methods for helping young people reinterpret what has happened to them is the art of asking good questions. How a question is posed determines the conclusion one reaches. For example, "Why is everyone out to get me?" has a pretty narrow response: "The fault lies with the rest of the world."

On the other hand, we can steer a kid toward asking, "What is it about how I come across that makes some people suspicious of me?" This yields a completely different conclusion. We might say to such a young person, "I know you're a great kid, but others are telling you by their responses that they're not seeing the real you, but someone who causes them to feel suspicious instead. Do you think that could be happening? What are some ways you could better communicate who you really are, so people can experience the real you?"

This approach of asking good questions minimizes power struggles and the need for kids to become defensive about who's good and bad, who's right or wrong. Others' responses don't need to be taken so personally; they're just feedback. At first, a young person may come up with defensive interpretations: "They're jerks," "They don't understand," "They don't care." Rather than arguing over that, an adult can say, "Okay, that's one possibility. What are some others?"

While it may be helpful for kids to understand what drives them to react as they do, it is not always necessary. When people realize that something is not working—that it's not giving them what they want—they tend to change their methods. So, instead of asking "Why in the world did you do that?!" pose the question, "How did that approach work for you?" The first question leads to a hundred dead ends. The second offers opportunity for reflection and change.

The same principle applies to frustrated adults working with kids in pain. The question, "What's wrong with this kid?" quickly shuts down possibilities. "What is it about how I have been coming across that keeps this kid resisting me?" opens up new avenues for connecting. Rather than asking, "Why won't this kid learn his lesson?" try asking, "What is about our approach that is motivating this kid to make destructive choices despite the consequences?"

Strategies for Confronting With Concern

We have been focusing on developing a sense of power in kids who feel powerless. But what about when kids abuse power? Responsibility requires that we confront those who abuse power over others. The word "confront" is easily misunderstood, since it has two possible definitions. It can mean to attack, as to confront in battle. But it also means to face something directly. The latter definition applies to building responsibility.

Youth who are comfortable with hurtful behavior are unlikely to change unless the reality of what they are doing becomes very clear. Some kids are not suffering from excess guilt, but from a lack of it. Only when they understand the effect their behavior has had on others, and how they have hurt themselves, will they be motivated to change. It's like the *Simpsons* episode when Bart destroys Lisa's Thanksgiving centerpiece. She asks him to look inside his heart and find the little place that knows he hurt his sister's feelings. He rolls his eyes and pretends to scan his heart: "Looking, looking, looking, not finding it, looking, looking . . ." Suddenly he pauses: "Uh oh."

Confrontation rooted in animosity or indifference never produces positive results. In fact, demeaning confrontation (attacking the person, rather than the behavior) fuels hostile relationships and climates. On the other hand, there is no more powerful method of discipline than to be respectfully confronted by persons who deeply care about you.

Nearly two hundred years ago, Swiss youth pioneer Johann Pestalozzi said that the crowning achievement of education was to be able to correct youth and in the same instant convince them of our fervent love. When confrontation is executed in respectful, caring ways, there is almost no concern that cannot be addressed. Even if youth do not immediately agree, they are not able to easily dismiss advice given in the spirit of genuine love by someone who has their best interests at heart.

The following techniques are helpful for confronting troubled kids, but also for teaching them how to confront others—even adults—in a constructive, nonaggressive fashion. To build on that a bit further, an essential part of giving power to kids is allowing them to appropriately express their criticisms toward us as adults, too. Kids need safe ways to verbalize and address points of disagreement with adults and other kids, and allowing them to practice this gives them a life skill that will serve them well in the future.

Apply Truth in Labeling

Youth engaged in problem behavior often brag about their rule-breaking, drug use, and alleged sexual conquests. Through a process called deviance coaching, they encourage one another in negative thinking, values, and acts. In deviance coaching, the definitions of "positive" and "negative" behaviors are swapped: Acts of kindness are labeled as "weak" and "sissy," and intimidation as "tough" and "macho."

Much of the language and music of contemporary youth subculture romanticize risky and deviant behavior. Slang gives drinking and drugs cool connotations by establishing a private lingo that confers belonging through its use: Kids brag about getting high, wasted, or baked. They castigate those kids who don't participate or hang out with adults as snitches or brown-nosers. They give assertive girls sexually demeaning labels and attack creative or sensitive boys with hostile homophobic terms.

Youth who try to protect vulnerable kids from bullying also become targets of ridicule. Crime is sanitized to appear victimless. No kid says, "I stole a purse from somebody's lonely grandmother"; that wouldn't be cool. Translated into macho language, the story becomes, "I ripped off that rich old lady." This celebration of deviance is like Newspeak propaganda and silences the voice of conscience.

Caring only becomes fashionable as hurting goes out of style. To stop such behavior, we must challenge the rhetoric that romanticizes it. But mentors need a method beyond moralistic condemnation.

The strategy of relabeling is designed to reveal the truth about hurting and helping. All acts of helping others are described in terms of strength and maturity, qualities youth naturally embrace. Similarly, all acts of hurting are relabeled as weak and immature, which youth naturally shun. Relabeling is a powerful method for using negative situations to unmask potential strengths of youth, as illustrated in the following examples:

Youth: Smoking pot's no big deal. I'm just having fun.

Mentor: Getting stoned just messes with your mind. Do you really believe that doing drugs is going to solve your problems or move you closer toward what you really want in life?

Youth: I'll skip school whenever I want. It's my life.

Mentor: Are you really still playing around with that hide-and-seek kid stuff? You seem so much smarter than that.

Youth: I'm too slick to get caught stealing.

Mentor: You mean you're too sneaky? Can your friends trust you not to steal their stuff?

Youth: Tony's just a snitch. I can't believe he ratted me out.

Mentor: Tony's got guts. He takes a stand when no one else will.

The foregoing examples may need to be adjusted to the linguistic code and slang of particular youth subcultures, but the process is basic. Mentors challenge the thinking that justifies hurting behavior and call on the positive strengths of youth.

But a caution is in order. Never attach pejorative labels to the *person,* only to the *behavior.* The message you want to send is, "This is a very immature way of acting for someone as smart as you," not, "You are so immature."

Sandwich Criticism

No one enjoys being criticized. Criticism is usually best received if balanced with positive messages. Another tip from Girls and Boys Town is the idea of a "sandwich" as a method for constructive correction: Every confrontational comment is preceded and followed by supportive ones. Begin with a statement conveying positive esteem or empathy; next, address the meat of the confrontation; finally, wrap up the sandwich with another message of esteem or empathy.

This is a very "brain friendly" method of confrontation: Since there's no verbal attack, the amygdala won't trigger the reptilian survival brain. Through sandwiching the confrontation with supportive statements in a nonthreatening manner, one engages the emotional and logical brain to consider the concern being raised, as in the following example.

> *Support:* Maria, you are really a powerful person in this group.

> *Confrontation:* I have noticed that sometimes you forget and say things that really hurt others by belittling or ridiculing them. Yesterday, I heard you tell Sarah and Megan that their ideas were stupid.

> *Support:* They look up to you, which is why they feel so hurt. You are a powerful role model for them.

As in all of the methods discussed in this chapter, your statements must not be scripted or insincere. Kids react more harshly to a canned method than almost anything else. And make sure that you compliment a kid at other times, not only just before you blast him or her, or your supportive statements will be rightly perceived as fake and inauthentic.

Ask, Don't Tell

Moralistic advice is perhaps the most overrated and overused method of building character in youth. The effective mentor models, guides, and stimulates, but tries to avoid preaching. This is particularly important in group discussions, since nothing kills genuine youth participation or invites adversarial contests like adult moralizing.

However, at times it is necessary for adults to put their ideas into play. The trick is to challenge youth's thinking without treating them as little kids or provoking a power contest. Never lecture without allowing or seeking input from youth.

People are by nature autonomous and don't like feeling controlled or bossed around. A wealth of research shows that directive comments trigger controlling counterreactions and interfere with learning and motivation.[10] Consider the Latin word *educaré*, from which the term "education" comes. It means "to draw out of." Surely Aristotle understood this when he introduced the method of dialectic questioning to help his students find answers themselves. This method has been called "ask, don't tell." Here are two examples that avoid lectures on manners and allow kids to correct themselves and feel in control of the group dynamic:

> *Several class members are talking at once, drowning out a highly perceptive comment by one youth.*
>
> Teacher: Did the group hear what Carla said?
>
> *One person is dominating a group discussion.*
>
> Facilitator: Does the group want John to take all the responsibility for running this group?

Should the group become hostile toward a member, the adult may have to intervene to ensure safety. Even here, a question may serve better than an authoritative command.

> *Peers are becoming frustrated with a member's resistance, and the tone becomes destructive.*
>
> Facilitator: What is happening now? Is the group going to allow Sheri to provoke them into treating her in the same way she's treating them?

This type of questioning keeps the group involved, yet allows the adult to have significant input as needed. One must be cautious, however, as questions can sometimes be more controlling than statements. Youth can quickly read through leading questions to the statement the adult really wants to make. The goal here is not to take charge of thinking, but instead to challenge youth to draw resources and responsibility from within themselves. As groups mature, the level of questioning by the adult diminishes, since group members learn to spot most issues themselves. Yet the adult always remains involved to support youth in their new-found responsibility.

Model How to Admit Mistakes

If we want kids to take an active role in apologizing and making amends, we have to show them how to handle it with respect for ourselves and for the injured party. Making amends does not mean groveling or losing face; it's a way of deepening connections.

We all know the ineffectiveness of the "do what I say, not what I do" approach to teaching kids. No one likes hypocrisy, and kids are especially sensitive to it. If we hope to instill in them a sense of responsibility for their actions and the ability to admit failure, then we must model that same stance. This is the essence of the Golden Rule. It applies not just to being kind or understanding in an easy, feel-good way, but also to toughing out the moments that are hard for us, but important to the other person.

Scott Larson recalls his interactions with one of the youth in their aftercare home.

> Shortly after we had opened our transitional home for kids coming out of lockup, I was talking to a friend on the phone. He asked me how things were going. "It's a lot tougher than I thought it would be," I confessed. "Just one of these guys can be a full-time job. I don't know how much more of this I can take."
>
> No sooner had the words left my mouth when I turned and saw Damion standing in the doorway of my office. He had heard every word. He whirled around and quickly left. By the look on his face, I knew I had hurt him deeply.
>
> I had to rush off to a conference where I was speaking, so I wasn't able to talk with Damion before leaving. All the while I was driving, I kept thinking about how my words had wounded him.
>
> Finally, I pulled over along the side of the road to phone him. "I'm so sorry for what I said on the telephone, Damion," I said. "I was just having a frustrating day. And I want you to know that I'm so glad that you are here. Will you forgive me for what I said?"
>
> He was quiet for a minute, then said, "Yes."

When we had first met Damion, he informed us there were three things he never said: "Please," "Thank you," and "I'm sorry." But after that experience, saying the words "I'm sorry" came much easier for him.

Some kids may not have experienced an adult apologizing to them, let alone asking for forgiveness; whatever happened has always been their fault. Perhaps adults fear undermining their authority by expressing culpability or weakness. The truth is, admitting our own errors to kids *strengthens* our credibility with them. When they realize that they are in a relationship of equality, in which either party has the power to hurt *and* the responsibility to heal, kids more readily step up to the plate.

Turn Bullies Into Positive Leaders

Most groups have one or more members who are highly skilled at conning or controlling others. These are not necessarily delinquents, but powerful and sometimes popular youth who psychologically or emotionally intimidate peers. Often these youth have an abundance of ill-gotten self-confidence from exerting power over others. Left unchecked, bullies wield destructive influence.

Our strategy is not to remove the bullying youth from the group, but to change the balance of leadership. In extreme situations, it may be necessary to remove a youth for a time, but this always must be a staff decision, rather than a peer decision. However, even a temporary timeout can be used as a teaching opportunity for the group, who may be charged with the task of helping prepare the young person for positive reentry.

In a typical school, less than 15 percent are active bullies, and a similar number are perpetual victims.[11] Widespread bullying has the most influence over the general audience. Often, a few onlookers become the cheering section for bullies, while a silent majority of bystanders enable bullying by their inaction.

It is generally unwise to criticize negative leaders in the presence of peers, since that only serves to give them more status and group support. Instead, privately confront such persons, embracing their strengths while inviting them to question why they need to bully others. Enlist them to be a positive force.

Mentor [confronting a tough kid about intimidation]: What happened in the hall with Jamie?

Youth: I was just showing him who is boss.

Mentor: Don't you think someone as strong as you could use your strength to build people up rather than tear them down?

Mobilizing the silent majority so that there is absolutely no support for ridicule or bullying in the broader group climate undermines and often extinguishes the bully's base of support. In effect, the intent is to box the bully into a bind so that if he or she hopes to be a leader, the only option is positive leadership.

Experience has shown that if handled well, these challenging youth can become the strongest positive members of the group. In positive peer climates, many former bullies have been transformed into leaders who now employ their strength to befriend and protect those who are vulnerable.

Victims also need to be given more confidence and may even need social-skills or assertiveness training. But they should not be expected to take on the bully directly. We can also recruit supporters for victimized students by challenging bystanders to halt any actions that support a negative leader's hurtful behavior.

The most effective social control of young people is not found in adult policing and harsh penalties, but in creating a culture where youth are empowered to take responsibility for one another. Young persons become the architects of their own responsible, caring community. As we shall see in the final chapter, having a sense of personal power is essential to having a sense of purpose within the community as a whole.

Endnotes

[1] Mandela 2003. Mandela used this quote from Marianne Williamson's "Our Deepest Fear" (*Return to Love*, 1992) in his inaugural address in 1995.

[2] Du Bois 1997, 200.

[3] Vorrath and Brendtro 1985.

[4] Fuller 2003, 21.

[5] Definitions adapted from Hanley 2005.

[6] This concept has been widely researched in psychology as "self-efficacy," a term first coined by Albert Bandura.

[7] These three principles were presented by Dr. Richard Curwin at the 2001 Black Hills Seminars in Rapid City, SD.

[8] Based upon material presented in Cline and Fay 1992, 146–147.

[9] Our discussions of these and the following methods draw liberally on *The EQUIP Program* (Gibbs, Potter, and Goldstein 1995) and *Positive Peer Culture* (Vorrath and Brendtro 1984).

[10] Deci and Flaste 1995.

[11] Hoover and Olsen 2001, 11–12.

chapter six

Instilling Purpose

It is despair, loneliness, and hopelessness. We need

someone to talk to; we need to be taught how to talk.

We need people who really care about us, support

us. . . . Teach us to hope. Bring some kind of meaning

and purpose to our lives.

—A high-school student[1]

The kids that come in front of me [in court] seldom focus their attention outside themselves. Most are self-centered all the time. Instead of just fining them and having them go to class, I've begun having them complete twenty hours of community service on their own.

The key is that they have to go find a place to serve other people in the community. We used to have a program where we would have them go clean up the school or something, but they did it just because the court made them. Here, they have to go find ways to serve.

One girl went to an animal shelter. Her mom was not too thrilled because she brought home about five dogs, but when she came back to me after having completed her ten hours, she was glowing. Her eyes were on fire. She said it was the most wonderful thing she had ever done; she loved it and was going to keep volunteering.

Another guy came in with the same kind of spark in his eye. He had called the Head Start program in his county and asked if they had anything he could do. He was only fifteen and didn't think he could do much for them. They told him to come on down, they had the perfect thing. They let him be the big brother to a four-year-old kid who had no brothers and sisters. That was it for this boy. Instead of hanging out as he used to, he's spending time with this younger kid at the Head Start center. His whole life changed.

I rule that these kids have to spend ten or twenty hours in service, and they end up doing it for months or more. Three or four non-profit agencies have written asking about the program, praising the kids.[2]

Many youth today feel that their presence makes little difference in the world. The kids doing community service in the preceding story were sent to court for shoplifting. Little did they know they would switch from thieving to giving.

One survey asked high-school students what they felt was the biggest problem with their generation. Their response: *Not having anything important to do.*[3]

Hans Selye, a pioneer in stress research, concluded that the ultimate antidote to life's stress is altruism: helping others in need without expecting any reward in return.[4] Seeing that others have greater needs than our own can help us reinterpret our own stories from a new perspective, one with more gratitude and appreciation for what we have received and achieved. Selye's research found that altruism even boosts the immune system and contributes to health and well-being.

The foundation of altruism is empathy, the basis for character and moral development. The antithesis of empathy is egotism, a self-centered existence that ignores the needs of others.

Identifying a Spiritual Destination

Scientific and spiritual worldviews converge in research on
resilience. While in the past, mixing spirituality and the social
sciences was taboo, today many research institutions are making
spirituality a critical component of their developmental science
departments.

Dr. Richard Lerner of Tufts University maintains, "The defining
characteristic of what it means to be human resides in the realm
of spirituality."[5] Harvard Psychiatrist Robert Coles agrees,
remarking how from earliest ages children ask the same eternal
questions as great thinkers like Tolstoy and Gaugin: "Where do
we come from? Who are we? Where are we going?"[6]

Youth whose lives are in pain and turmoil are even more likely to
pose deeply spiritual questions like, "Why was I even born?"
and "What is the reason to go on living?" Sadly, those who wres-
tle most with such weighty issues often have the fewest opportunities to explore them, as many youth professionals are taught to
run from such discussions.

Sometimes spiritual questions stem from a sense of pain and
hopelessness, but when young people become committed to caring for others, soul-searching can also lead to transformation.
They begin to ask questions like, "What kind of person do I want
to be? What impact do I want to have on others and the world?
What do I want my life to amount to?"

Following is an entry from a journal written by seventeen-year-
old Tyrone during a period of serious reflection about the meaning of his life. In the entry, Tyrone is painfully aware of how he
has hurt others. While before he wanted to die, he comes to realize that he has actually been living a kind of spiritual death. We
see inklings of his desire to change, even though he is not quite
there yet:

> A lot of times I think I'm dead. You might as well
> say I am. The only difference in being dead is I feel
> I would be a lot better off at times. Not having to
> worry about going out and hurting someone.
> Getting into trouble, even to the point of getting

locked up. A lot of times I don't even know why God put me on the earth. I don't feel like I've accomplished anything but hurting people.

This is a spiritual cry, and caregivers who are products of an era when such issues were seldom mentioned may be uncertain of how to respond. Young persons like Tyrone are in desperate need of opportunities to discover purpose in their lives. When youth become committed to selfless serving of others, however, a spiritual passion often emerges in them. Community service activities and person-to-person helping projects do have a powerful role-reversing effect on once irresponsible and antisocial youth.

A final notation in Tyrone's journal reveals this hunger to be of value to others. At this point, one sees a profound shift in his reasoning. He is no longer preoccupied with self-centered thinking, but is beginning to reach out to help others, even as he continues to reconstruct his life:

> What I would like to do is be able to go and talk to young kids who want to run around with gangs and guns, steal, disobey their parents, or just skip school. I would like to talk to some of the kids before it gets too late and they end up where I am right now. I feel I can do a lot for them. I feel like I've done enough to some kids in the negative way, and I'd like to do some positive for them.

After this was written, Tyrone became highly motivated. He completed his GED, worked to rebuild his relationships with his family, and was paroled from the institution to take a job in the community. The last time we saw Tyrone, he was talking of saving his money for college. While his problems are not over, the trajectory of his life seems to have been altered.

Experience with thousands of youth in peer-helping and service-learning programs suggests that decentering—breaking free from self-preoccupation—is essential for antisocial youth to move into prosocial lifestyles.

All people have a powerful predisposition toward altruism, but this must be cultivated in each child. It is not enough to focus on correcting deviance; we must build strengths and immerse youth in a culture of helping. Young persons who reach out to others discover new proof of their worthiness, for they are now of value to someone else.

Breaking With the Past

Many believe the core pathology of modern society lies in the loss of a sense of shared community. This is the attraction of the gang for many youth who are not positively bonded to caring adults. In fact, if we did not have a deep need for sharing and self-sacrifice, gangs would not even exist.

But what about when a young person's primary bonds have been to abusive persons? One important step toward exercising responsibility is to cease being under the control of earlier abusive experiences or relationships. For some kids, it may be difficult to admit the abuse, much less separate from abusers. Children who defend, conceal, and compensate for their parents' addictions, for example, need help finding appropriate ways to express their anger, ways that don't require them to deny caring about the only family they have.

Part of this process of making a healthy separation from abusive environments involves forgiving those who have inflicted harm. Forgiveness does not necessarily mean forgetting the past or trusting the offender again in the future. But it does break the destructive bond that keeps a victim held perpetually hostage. As someone once said, "Holding onto hatred is like preparing a cup of poison for your enemy, then drinking it yourself."

To develop into healthy, resilient adults, young persons cannot forever remain prisoners of earlier damaging relationships maintained through the bond of hatred. Of course, simply expecting a child to detach from whatever has held them previously—even if it is destructive—is unrealistic. We must provide new models of positive bonding and experiences that build character and purpose. As we have seen, as adults we can provide some of those powerful new connections with kids who need us; the next step for those kids is to "pass it on," to make their own powerful and empowering connections with others who need them.

Strategies for Making Caring Cool

How do we get self-centered youth hooked on helping? Caring is not fashionable among many youth in modern culture. Youth who are weakly bonded to adults lack mentors for building positive values. As a result, many gravitate to negative youth subcultures, where they become trapped in self-centered, exploitative lifestyles. Angry and lacking hope and purpose, they neither respect themselves nor others.

To transform such youth requires tapping their positive potential and innate ability to show concern for others. Following are some practical methods for making caring fashionable among young people.

To nurture a sense of purpose, youth must be given opportunities to serve. In recent years, this enduring principle has been put into the practice in thousands of schools. Fifteen million youth participate in volunteer activities that integrate service with the curriculum. Eight out of ten principals in schools offering service learning say it has a positive impact on school climate, academic achievement, and teacher satisfaction.[7] Perhaps most significantly, it meets needs all young persons have to make contributions to others.

Service is beneficial not just to youth, but also, if activities are meaningful, to the community. For example, one night per week, youth from Straight Ahead Ministries' residential program feed the homeless on the streets of Boston. This benefits both the homeless, as well as those who serve.

After his first time out, Shawn said, "Wow, I used to kick those guys when I'd walk by them on the streets, and tonight I was giving them food and getting to know them. After tonight, I know I'll never treat a street person the way I used to."

The involvement of idealistic young people in service learning is a natural match between their strong desire to be of value and the pressing needs of our society. Yet many schools and traditional youth organizations have failed to recognize that troubled adolescents have strong needs for service and much to offer.

Students at Starr Commonwealth in Michigan and Ohio carry out more than one hundred community service projects each year, from tutoring young children to participating in a horsemanship program for disabled children. Many service-learning activities are integrated into the curriculum, as seen by these examples:

- Creative-arts students studied clowning and drama, which led to a series of clowning performances for children in a community daycare center.

- Social-science students studied the process of aging by gathering oral histories from residents in an extended-care facility. They formed strong bonds. Some continued volunteer work and began considering health service careers.

- An industrial technology class built a picnic pavilion for the Campfire Girls, which turned out to be a particularly complex project.

- English literature students read an essay titled "The Gift," then, for homework, gave a gift and wrote about the experience. One student wrote: "It was the first time I had ever done anything I wasn't paid for."

Yet service-learning programs must surmount a formidable obstacle with some self-centered students, who may ridicule values of service or giving of self to others. Instead, such students place a premium on toughness, autonomy, daring, and the ability to exploit others. Always needing to appear strong, they feel vulnerable to criticism from peers if they should show their gentler, more positive side.

To overcome egocentrism, youth must have some overall commitment to something beyond themselves. One place to begin is by making the connection of how their actions affect their mother, grandmother, or younger siblings. That often hits a soft spot.

Appeal to Their Interests

Service-learning programs can also capture the commitment of troubled teenagers by appealing to their interests. For example, kids are more receptive to approaches that reinforce their maturity

("You can be of real help to these people") than those that maintain their dependence ("This will straighten you out"). Helping others also needs to be seen as an act of strength ("This will be a tough job"), rather than of weakness ("This should be easy enough for you").

Don't Force It

Straight Ahead Ministries' most successful community program for youth released from juvenile facilities is community service. While many delinquent youth have court-mandated community service requirements, they cannot count the work they do with the homeless in Straight Ahead's program toward those hours.

"We want kids who are there for the homeless, not for themselves," says the program director. "We don't want them to see community service as a punishment, but as a privilege." To be involved, kids must make a ten-week commitment that includes two weeks of training to promote a better understanding of the homeless. Skeptics might be surprised to learn that there is a long waiting list for kids to get into the program. "It seems the higher we raise the bar, the more takers we have," the project coordinator observes.

Give Them a Thrill

Service projects must be seen as exciting and spontaneous, rather than routine and regimented. Pioneer social worker Jane Addams observed that many youth get into trouble because of their strong appetites for excitement and adventure. Highly adventurous projects (such as building levees to stop a flood) may be rare, but it is possible to eschew repetitive helping projects for projects with variety and challenge.

So often we focus on getting kids to say "no" to many things. But it's when they find the big "yes" that things really begin to change for them. When we provide projects that tap into a young person's passion, big things happen. As one youth returning from a week-long volunteer service project of helping physically handicapped adults exclaimed, "I finally found the reason I was born!" Suddenly this young man had something bigger to live for than mere self-gratification. Now, nine years later, he is the director of a program that works with juvenile offenders to serve disabled adults.

This was also the lesson for five boys from Youth off the Streets in Sydney, Australia. Each of them had grown up in painful situations that included physical and sexual abuse and sometimes even the murder of a parent. They reacted to pain by turning to alcohol or drug abuse, living on the dangerous streets of Sydney where one survives by crime, violence, and selling drugs or oneself.

Part of the requirement for coming to Youth off the Streets is to give back to society. "It is vitally important for these troubled youth to be able to shrug off their victim mentality," says Father Chris Riley, founder of the program.

This group of boys decided to visit an orphanage in East Timor that had been torn by war and poverty. There was no running water, and children received only one meal per day. The boys planned the trip and raised all of the funds needed to get there and present three different orphanages with two thousand dollars each. Here are some of the reflections from these "troubled" boys:

> *Joseph: Living in a country like Australia and going to East Timor is a big reality check, because it makes you realize that you shouldn't take things for granted. One of the greatest lessons I learned was that everyone can make a difference if given the proper challenges in life.*

> *Luke: This experience will help me realize that I can't always get what I want, and to put others before myself.*

> *Ian: When I wake in the morning, I worry about what to wear; they worry about what to eat. This taught me a lot about generosity.*

> *Beau: The people there are so happy and willing to help. We might have our own problems, but there are people out there who are a lot worse off.*

Will: This was the most powerful thing I have ever experienced. I'll never be the same.

There are now many more youth from Australia's Youth off the Streets program who can't wait to make the next trip to East Timor. Truly, there is no higher expression of humanity than to be able to give to others and, in so doing, to transform one's own life. Five boys from Sydney were allowed that experience, and two hundred orphans in East Timor will not forget it, either.

Looking Forward on Our Journey

Recently we were talking with a group of kids in a detention center about what it takes to really make it out in the world. Most of them had already given up on that prospect. They recited all the things that kept sidetracking them from what they really wanted—drugs, crime, fighting, gang activity—the list went on and on.

Finally we interrupted and asked, "So what is it you really want?"

Tony responded first: "To not get locked up again."

Others chimed in with, "To quit doing drugs," "To get back into school again," "To live a good life," and "To stop having so many problems."

"Okay . . . ," we said, "it's clear what you *don't* want, but what is it you really *do* want?"

This turned out to be a much more difficult question for the kids to answer. It was a shift from the typical conversation they had been engaged in that focused on what they were doing wrong and what wasn't working. They had become pretty clear on those issues, but being asked to examine what they wanted—as more than the mere absence of negatives—posed a real dilemma.

As the group examined this problem, we talked about how when you're focused on something that's positive, you're not focused on all the negative things—and how the negative things often end up taking care of themselves. Sixteen-year-old Nick came up with a great analogy: "So, when we say we want to do good, but we're always looking back at the things that have tripped us up, it's sort of like trying to ride a bike while looking backwards?"

Nick captured the essence of resilience. Resilience demands focusing on what we believe *can* happen in kids' lives, rather than on what's not happening or what's happening poorly.

We foster resilience in kids when we foster resilience in our-selves—when we suspend our *own* tit-for-tat urge to win and proactively provide what is really needed instead of merely returning pain for pain. We gain their respect and trust by offer-ing our *own* respect and trust, by responding to the inside kid, rather than reacting to an outside facade. We feed their hunger to feel competent by showing them their strengths, rather than constantly pointing out their weaknesses. We empower kids toward greatness by overriding our propensity toward control. We encourage responsibility by creating environments that reward kids for courage and risk-taking, rather than force or pun-ish them into submission and mediocrity.

And perhaps most of all, we change kids' lives by believing (in spite of "evidence" to the contrary) that kids really do want to make it. They are trying to make the best choices they can, given their experience and understanding of the world. We show how many other choices and possibilities exist by first believing that those possibilities exist in and for our most challenging kids. Our hope is that after reading this book, you will put that belief to the test by actively engaging with kids in new ways that promote transformational change—not only in them, but in yourself.

Endnotes

[1] These remarks are from a high-school boy speaking at a school assem-bly following the suicide of a classmate. The student went on to say that they all needed to confront the real problems underneath suicide and drug and alcohol abuse. Cited in Varenhorst 2004, 130.

[2] Hanley 1989, 85.

[3] Survey conducted and cited by Guy Doud in a general session at Youth Specialties National Youth Workers Convention in Chicago in October, 1988.

[4] Selye 1978.

[5] From a presentation at *Spirituality: Its Role in Child and Youth Development,* a conference at Tufts University in November 2003.

[6] Coles 1990, 299.

[7] Kielsmeier, Scales, Roehlkepartain, and Neal 2004.

Appendix

Learning-Style Indicator

© **Dell Coats Erwin. Adapted and used with permission.**

This indicator was developed by Dell Coats Erwin and is based on Dr. Howard Gardner's work on multiple intelligences. To some degree, everyone has strengths in all nine intelligences, but most people are stronger in one or more areas. Knowing where young people are strong can help those who work with them better understand and more appropriately assist them. Knowing their own strengths can also help young people better understand and appreciate themselves. Likewise, understanding where a youth is not strong can reveal areas that need work. The more a young person learns and grows, the stronger he or she will become in each area.

The following assessment is for youth to self-administer. It's not a diagnostic test, but rather a way to have fun while opening up new learning and self-discovery. Before passing out the assessment, take some time to explain that every person is intelligent in all nine areas to some degree, and that each of us also has preferences, ways in which we learn best. Discuss how discovering our preferences can be fun and helpful when it comes to such things as career planning, and point out how discovering which types of learning are not as comfortable can help us grow stronger in those as well.

This simple indicator is not comprehensive and only provides clues regarding strengths in each intelligence. One weakness of this assessment is that it is conducted mainly through the linguistic intelligence. The best way to assess different forms of intelligence may be through observation of performance and activities based on each intelligence. For more complete assessments, visit the web, keying "Multiple Intelligences Assessments" into your search engine.

Appendix Learning-Style Indicator

Nine Ways to be Smart

© **Dell Coats Erwin. Adapted and used with permission.**

This worksheet is based on the ideas of Howard Gardner, a Harvard psychologist. He calls the nine ways to be smart "multiple intelligences." They may also be thought of as learning styles and preferences.

Everyone is smart in all nine ways to some degree. But you may be stronger in one or more of them. Knowing where you are strongest can help you understand yourself better and learn better. Knowing where you are not as strong can show you areas to work on. As you learn and grow, you will become stronger in each area.

One way to be smart is NOT better than another, just different!

Name: _____

Directions: Put a check beside each statement that is true about you.

1. *Word Smart (Linguistic Intelligence)*

_____ Like to write

_____ Use words well when speaking

_____ Enjoy telling stories and jokes

_____ Have a good memory for names, places, dates, and other information

_____ Enjoy reading

_____ Like poems, puns, and tongue twisters

_____ Like word activities like Scrabble®, anagrams, crossword puzzles, and so on

_____ Like to speak in front of groups

_____ Find it easy to explain ideas to others

_____ Often contact friends through notes and letters

2. *Thinking/Numbers Smart (Logical-Mathematical Intelligence)*

_____ Think things out clearly   *141*

_____ Can do math in head

_____ Enjoy using computers

_____ Like chess and checkers

_____ Like to do experiments

_____ Like working on thinking puzzles

_____ Keep things neat and orderly

_____ Like step-by-step directions

_____ Like structure

_____ Find it easy to solve problems

3. *Pictures/Images Smart (Spatial Intelligence)*

_____ Like pictures and other visuals

_____ See pictures in mind when thinking

_____ Like mazes, jigsaw puzzles, and Lego® blocks

_____ Enjoy drawing and designing things

_____ Like maps and charts

_____ Daydream a lot

_____ Like creating art using different tools: chalk, paint, or markers

_____ Like to rearrange a room

_____ Like watching plays, musicals, and other performances

_____ Can remember the way a room looks and feels

4. *Music Smart (Musical Intelligence)*

_____ Enjoy music a lot

_____ Often sing, hum, or whistle songs to themselves

_____ Play musical instrument or sing in a choir

_____ Hear sounds others may miss—bells ringing far away, birds, crickets

_____ Like to have music playing all the time

_____ Find it hard to concentrate while listening to the radio or TV

_____ Have good rhythm to music

Appendix Learning-Style Indicator

_____ Like the rhythms of poetry

_____ Like musicals better than dramatic plays

_____ Find it easy to remember words of songs

5. *Body Smart (Kinesthetic Intelligence)*

_____ Cleverly mimic other people's movements and behaviors

_____ Enjoy taking part in sports

_____ Like to dance, act, do aerobics, martial arts, or miming

_____ Move a lot when sitting on a chair

_____ Like physical activities such as hiking, swimming, biking, or skating

_____ Am good with woodworking, sewing, or carving

_____ Enjoy making things with hands

_____ Like working with tools

_____ Find it hard to sit still for long periods

_____ Enjoy arts and crafts

6. *People Smart (Interpersonal Intelligence)*

_____ Am a leader in the neighborhood or at school

_____ Understand people very well

_____ Have a lot of friends

_____ Like to be with people

_____ Try to solve disputes

_____ Enjoy group games and/or group events

_____ Care a lot about people and their feelings

_____ Learn and perform best when working with others

_____ Dislike working alone

_____ Like belonging to clubs and other groups

7. *Self Smart (Intrapersonal Intelligence)*

_____ Am deeply aware of inner feelings and thoughts

_____ Have strong personality and will

_____ Like to work on projects alone

The Resilience Revolution © 2006 Solution Tree (formerly National Educational Service)
www.solution-tree.com

_____ Seem to live in own private, inner world

_____ Have self-confidence

_____ Act very different in style of dress and behavior

_____ Put out a lot of effort when I believe in something

_____ Like to be involved in causes that help others

_____ Am very aware of what I believe

_____ Believe that fairness is very important

8.   *Nature Smart (Naturalist Intelligence)*

_____ Care deeply about animals

_____ When outside, closely notice sky, clouds, and plants

_____ Enjoy growing plants

_____ Like collecting rocks and seashells

_____ Like going to the beach or walking in the woods

_____ Like to watch fish in an aquarium for a long time

_____ Care very much about the environment and endangered species

_____ Believe it is very important to recycle

_____ Enjoy hiking and camping

_____ Spend a lot of time outdoors

9.   *Deep-Thoughts Smart (Existential Intelligence)*

_____ Ask lots of questions that start with "Why?" and "How?"

_____ Like to think about why things happen as they do

_____ Ask questions about why I and others were born

_____ Wonder a lot about why people die

_____ Think a lot about God and heaven

_____ Like to read and learn about the meaning of life

_____ Like to read the Bible, other religious books, or both

_____ Like to listen to sermons, discuss deep subjects, or both

_____ Like to go to religious services and events

_____ Like to pray in ways that involve talking to and listening to God

Appendix Learning-Style Indicator

Totals for All Nine Ways of Being Smart

144

1. _____ Word smart *(linguistic intelligence)*

2. _____ Thinking/numbers smart *(logical-mathematical intelligence)*

3. _____ Pictures/images smart *(spatial intelligence)*

4. _____ Music smart *(musical intelligence)*

5. _____ Body smart *(kinesthetic intelligence)*

6. _____ People smart *(interpersonal intelligence)*

7. _____ Self smart *(intrapersonal intelligence)*

8. _____ Nature smart *(naturalist intelligence)*

9. _____ Deep-thoughts smart *(existential intelligence)*

Meaning of Scores

This is not a test, and the scores are not like grades. You cannot make a good or a bad score. You may be high in some and low in some. That's true for most people. The scores will just help you to know yourself better.

You are smart in all nine ways. But you may shine in some of them. In those you will have the highest scores. You may want to complete this indicator each year to see how you may have changed.

Bibliography

Aggleton, J. P., ed. 2000. *The Amygdala: A Functional Analysis.* Oxford, UK: Oxford University Press.

Allport, Gordon. 1954. *The Nature of Prejudice.* Reading, MA: Addison-Wesley.

Anglin, James. 2003. *Pain, Normality, and the Struggle for Congruence: Reinterpreting Residential Care for Children and Youth.* Binghamton, NY: Haworth Press.

APPC [Annenberg Public Policy Center]. 2004. Adolescent Mental Health Initiative. University of Pennsylvania. Available at www.sunnylands.org/amhi/ (accessed October 13, 2005).

Armstrong, Thomas. 1997. *The Myth of the A.D.D. Child: 50 Ways to Improve Your Child's Behavior and Attention Span Without Drugs, Labels, or Coercion.* New York: Plume.

Bandura, Albert. 1995. Exercise of Personal and Collective Efficacy in Changing Societies. In *Self-Efficacy and Changing Societies,* edited by Albert Bandura, 1–45. New York: Cambridge University Press.

Barber, Brian K., ed. 2002. *Intrusive Parenting: How Psychological Control Affects Children and Adolescents.* Washington, DC: American Psychological Association.

Barnett, S., S. dos Reis, M. Riddle, and the Maryland Youth Practice Improvement Committee for Mental Health. 2002. Improving the Management of Acute Aggression in State Residential and Inpatient Psychiatric Facilities for Youths. *Child and Adolescent Psychiatry* 41 (8): 897–905.

Baumeister, R. F., and M. R. Leary. 1995. The Need to Belong: Desire for Interpersonal Attachments as a Fundamental Human Motivation. *Psychological Bulletin* 117: 479–529.

Beck, Aaron. 1999. *Prisoners of Hate: The Cognitive Basis of Anger, Hostility, and Violence.* New York: Harper Collins.

Beiser, Vince, and Angie Cannon. 2004 (August 9). Juvenile Injustice. *U.S. News & World Report* 137 (4): 28–32.

Benard, Bonnie. 2004. *Resiliency: What We Have Learned.* San Francisco: WestEd.

Benson, E. 2003. Researchers Are Still Looking for Consensus on How and When Anger First Appears in Infants. *Monitor on Psychology* 34 (3): 50–51.

Bettelheim, Bruno. 1974. *A Home for the Heart*. London: Thames and Hudson.

Blanchard, Geral. 1995. *The Difficult Connection*. Brandon, VT: Safer Society Press.

Brendtro, Larry, Martin Brokenleg, and Steve Van Bockern. 2002. *Reclaiming Youth at Risk: Our Hope for the Future*. Rev. ed. Bloomington, IN: Solution Tree (formerly National Educational Service).

Brendtro, Larry, and Lesley du Toit. 2005. *Response Ability Pathways*. Cape Town, South Africa: Pretext Publishers.

Brendtro, Larry, Arlin Ness, and Martin Mitchell. 2005. *No Disposable Kids*. Bloomington, IN: Solution Tree (formerly National Educational Service).

Brown, Brooks, and Rob Merritt. 2002. *No Easy Answers: The Truth Behind Death at Columbine High School*. New York: Lantern Books.

Brownlee, Shannon, Roberta Hotinski, Bellamy Pailthorp, Erin Ragan, and Kathleen Wong. 1999 (August 9). Inside the Teen Brain. *U.S. News & World Report* 127 (5): 44–53.

Brunk, Conrad G. 2001. Restorative Justice and the Philosophical Theories of Criminal Punishment. In *The Spiritual Roots of Restorative Justice*, edited by M. L. Hadley, 31–56. Albany, NY: State University of New York Press.

Buetler, Larry, and Mary Malik, eds. 2002. *Rethinking DSM*. Washington, DC: American Psychological Association.

Burke, Theta. 1976. *I've Heard Your Feelings*. Ann Arbor, MI: Delafield Press.

Cambone, Joseph. 1994. *Teaching Troubled Children*. New York: Teachers College Press.

Carroll, Lewis. [1866] 2002. *Alice's Adventures in Wonderland and Through the Looking Glass*. New York: Random House.

Cassidy, Jude, and Shaver, Phillip. 1999. *Handbook of Attachment: Theory, Research, and Clinical Applications*. New York: Guilford Press.

Clarke, Jean Illsley. 1999. *Connections: The Threads That Strengthen Families*. Center City, MN: Hazelden.

Cline, Foster W., and Jim Fay. 1992. *Parenting Teens With Love and Logic: Preparing Adolescents for Responsible Adulthood*. Colorado Springs, CO: Piñon Press.

Cobb, S. 1976. Social Support as a Moderator of Life Stress. *Psychosomatic Medicine* 38: 300–314.

Coles, Robert. 1990. *The Spiritual Life of Children*. Boston: Houghton-Mifflin.

Coopersmith, Stanley. 1967. *The Antecedents of Self-Esteem*. San Francisco: W. H. Freeman.

Csikszentmihalyi, Mihaly, Kevin Rathunde, and Samuel Whalen. 1993. *Talented Teenagers*. Melbourne, Australia: Cambridge University Press.

De Becker, Gavin. 1998. *The Gift of Fear*. New York: Dell.

Deci, Edward, and Richard Flaste. 1995. *Why We Do What We Do: The Dynamics of Personal Autonomy*. New York: G. Putnam's Sons.

De Mello, Anthony. 1992. *The Way to Love*. New York: Doubleday.

Desetta, Al, and Sybil Wolin, eds. 2000. *The Struggle to Be Strong*. Minneapolis, MN: Free Spirit.

Dewey, John. [1910] 1960. *How We Think*. Lexington, MA: Heath.

Diel, Paul. 1987. *The Psychology of Re-education*. Translated by Raymond Rosenthal. Boston: Shambhala.

Dishion, Thomas J., and Kate Kavanagh. 2003. *Intervening in Adolescent Problem Behavior: A Family-Centered Approach*. New York: Guilford Press.

Dodge, K., and D. Somberg. 1987. Hostile Attribution Biases Among Aggressive Boys Are Exacerbated Under Conditions of Threat to the Self. *Child Development* 58: 213–234.

Donovan, J., R. Jesser, and S. Costa. 1988. Syndrome of Problem Behavior in Adolescents. A Replication. *Journal of Consulting and Clinical Psychology* 56: 762–765.

Du Bois, W. E. B. 1997. *John Brown: A Biography*. A new edition with primary documents and introduction by John David Smith. Armonk, NY: M. E. Sharpe, Inc.

Eisenberger, N., M. Lieberman, and K. Williams. 2003. Does Rejection Hurt? An MRI Study of Social Exclusion. *Science* 302: 290–292.

Elshtain, Jean B. 2002. *The Jane Addams Reader*. New York: Basic Books.

Farley, Christopher John, and James Willwerth. 1998 (January 19). Dead Teen Walking. *Time* 151 (2): 50–57.

Flach, Frederic. 1989. *Resilience: Discovering a New Strength at Times of Stress*. New York: Fawcett Columbine.

Ford, Donald. H. 1994. *Humans as Self-Constructing, Living Systems: A Developmental Perspective on Behavior and Personality.* State College, PA: Ideals, Inc.

Fuller, Robert W. 2003. *Somebodies and Nobodies: Overcoming the Abuse of Rank.* Gabriola Island, Canada: New Society Publishers.

Gardner, Howard. 2000. *Intelligence Reframed: Multiple Intelligences for the 21st Century.* New York: Basic Books.

Gibbs, John. 1994. Fairness and Empathy as the Foundation for Universal and Moral Education. *Comenius* 14: 12–23.

Gibbs, John C., Granville Potter, and Arnold P. Goldstein. 1995. *The EQUIP Program: Teaching Youth to Think and Act Responsibly Through a Peer-Helping Approach.* Champaign, IL: Research Press.

Gladwell, Malcolm. 2005. *Blink: The Power of Thinking Without Thinking.* New York: Little, Brown.

Gold, M. 1995. Charting a Course: Promise and Prospects for Alternative Schools. *Journal of Emotional and Behavioral Problems* 3 (4): 8–11.

Gold, Martin, and David W. Mann. 1984. *Expelled to a Friendlier Place: A Study of Effective Alternative Schools.* Ann Arbor: University of Michigan Press.

Gold, Martin, and D. Wayne Osgood. 1992. *Personality and Peer Influence in Juvenile Corrections.* Westport, CT: Greenwood Press.

Goldstein, Arnold P. 1993. Interpersonal Skills Training Intervention. In *The Gang Intervention Handbook,* edited by Arnold P. Goldstein and C. R. Huff, 87–157. Champaign, IL: Research Press.

Goldstein, Arnold P., and Brian K. Martens. 2000. *Lasting Change: Methods for Enhancing Generalization of Gain.* Champaign, IL: Research Press.

Goleman, Daniel. 1995. *Emotional Intelligence.* New York: Bantam Books.

Gottman, John. 2001. *The Relationship Cure: A 5 Step Guide to Strengthening Your Marriage, Family, and Friendships.* New York: Three Rivers Press.

Greenspan, Stanley I. 1995. *The Challenging Child.* Reading, MA: Addison-Wesley.

Greenspan, Stanley I. 1997. *The Growth of the Mind and the Endangered Origins of Intelligence.* Cambridge, MA: Perseus Books.

Hall, Stephen S. 1999 (August 22). The Bully in the Mirror. *New York Times Magazine* 148: 35.

Hall, Samuel Read. [1829] 1973. *Lectures on School-Keeping.* Boston: Richardson, Lord and Holbrook.

Hallowell, E. 2002 (May 31). *Connections.* Paper presented at the National Adolescent Conference at the Ben Franklin Institute in Scottsdale, Arizona.

Hanley, John. 1989. *LifeSpring: Getting Yourself From Where You Are to Where You Want to Be.* New York: Simon and Schuster.

Hanley, John Jr. 2005. *Full-Tilt Boogie: Essential Coaching for Living Full-Blast.* Philadelphia, PA: Xlibris Corporation.

Harlow, H. F. 1958. The Nature of Love. *American Psychologist* 13: 673–685.

Hersch, Patricia. 1998. *A Tribe Apart: A Journey Into the Heart of American Adolescence.* New York: Fawcett Columbine.

Higgins, Gina O'Collins. 1994. *Resilient Adults: Overcoming a Cruel Past.* San Francisco: Jossey-Bass.

Hoffman, M. 2002. Toward a Comprehensive, Empathy-Based Theory of Pro-Social Development. In *Constructive and Destructive Behavior: Implications for Family, School, and Society,* edited by Arthur Bohart and Deborah Stipek, 61–86. Washington, DC: American Psychological Association.

Hoge, Warren. 2003. In Finnish Prisons, No Gates or Armed Guards. *New York Times* international edition, January 6.

Hoover, John, and Glenn Olsen. 2001. *Teasing and Harassment: The Frames and Scripts Approach for Teachers and Parents.* Bloomington, IN: Solution Tree (formerly National Educational Service).

Huff, Barbara. 2000. *Claiming Children.* Alexandria, VA: Federation of Families for Children's Mental Health. For more information, visit www.ffcmh.org (accessed September 14, 2005).

Huizinga, Johan. 2001. *Erasmus and the Age of Reformation.* Mineola, NY: Dover Publications.

Hunt, Morton. 1990. *The Compassionate Beast: What Science is Discovering About the Humane Side of Humankind.* New York: William Morrow and Company.

Hyman, Irwin, and Pamela Snook. 1999. *Dangerous Schools: What We Can Do About the Physical and Emotional Abuse of Our Children.* San Francisco: Jossey-Bass.

Hyman, Irwin, and Pamela Snook. 2001. Dangerous schools, alienated students. *Reclaiming Children and Youth* 10 (3): 133–136.

Johnson, S. 2003. Emotions and the Brain. *Discover* 24 (4): 62–69.

Key, Ellen. 1909. *The Century of the Child*. New York: G. P. Putnam's Sons.

KidsPeace. 1998. National Early Teen Survey. Orefield, PA: KidsPeace, Inc. www.kidspeace.org (accessed October 13, 2005).

Kielsmeier, James, Peter Scales, Eugene Roehlkepartain, and Marybeth Neal. 2004. Community Service and Service-Learning in Public Schools. *Reclaiming Children and Youth* 13 (3): 138–143.

Kilpatrick, William H. 1928. *Education for a Changing Civilization*. New York: MacMillan Company.

Knitzer, Jane, Zina Steinberg, and Brahm Fleisch. 1990. *At the Schoolhouse Door: An Examination of Programs and Policies for Children With Behavioral and Emotional Problems*. New York: Bankstreet College of Education.

Kohn, Alfie. 1990. *The Brighter Side of Human Nature: Altruism and Empathy in Everyday Life*. New York: Basic Books.

Korczak, Janusz. 1967. *Janusz Korczak: Collected Works*. Warsaw, Poland: United Nations.

Kozart, M. 2002. Understanding Efficacy and Psychotherapy: An Ethnomethodological Perspective on the Therapeutic Alliance. *American Journal of Orthopsychiatry* 72 (2): 217–231.

Kusche, Carol A., and M. T. Greenberg. 1994. *The PATHS Curriculum*. Seattle, WA: Developmental Research and Programs.

Lantieri, Linda, and Janet Patti. 1996. *Waging Peace in Our Schools*. Boston: Beacon Press.

LD Online. n.d. *Tell Me the Facts About Learning Disabilities*. Washington, DC: National Joint Committee on Learning Disabilities. Available at www.ldonline.org/ccldinfo (accessed September 14, 2005).

Lewis, Thomas, Fari Amini, and Richard Lannon. [2000] 2001. *A General Theory of Love*. New York: Vintage.

Lickona, T. 2001. What Good Is Character and How Can We Develop It in Our Children? *Reclaiming Children and Youth* 9 (4): 239–251.

Liepmann, Moritz. 1928. Die Selbstveranstaltung der Gefangenen. In *Hamburgische Schriften zur Gesamten Strafrechtswissenschaft* (vol. 12), edited by Moritz Liepmann. Berlin: Mannheim.

Long, Nicholas. 1995. Why Adults Strike Back. *Reclaiming Children and Youth* 4 (1): 11–15.

Long, Nicholas. 1997. The Therapeutic Power of Kindness. *Reclaiming Children and Youth* 5 (4): 242–246.

Long, Nicholas, and B. Dufner. 1980. The Stress Cycle or the Coping Cycle: The Impact of Home and School Stresses on Pupil's Classroom Behavior. In *Conflict in the Classroom* (4th ed.), edited by Nicholas Long, W. C. Morse, and R. G. Newman, 218–228. Belmont, CA: Wadsworth Publishing Company.

Long, Nicholas, Mary Wood, and Frank Fecser. 2001. *Life Space Crisis Intervention: Talking With Students in Conflict.* Austin, TX: Pro-Ed.

Lynch, James J. 1977. *The Broken Heart: The Medical Consequences of Loneliness.* New York: Basic Books.

Mandela, Nelson. 2003. A Fabric of Care. In *Nelson Mandela: From Freedom to the Future,* edited by Kader Asmal, David Chidester, and Wilmot James, 416–418. Johannesburg: Jonathan Ball Publishers.

Maslow, Abraham. 1970. *Motivation and Personality* (rev. ed.). New York: Harper & Row.

Mathur, S. R., and R. B. Rutherford. 1996. Is Social Skills Training Effective for Students With Emotional and Behavioral Disorders? Research Issues and Needs. *Behavioral Disorders* 22: 21–28.

Mayer, John, Peter Salovey, and David Caruso. 2000. Models of Emotional Intelligence. In *The Handbook of Intelligence,* edited by Robert J. Sternberg, 396–422. Cambridge, MA: Yale University Press.

McClellan, Jon M., and John Scott Werry. 2000. Introduction: Research on Psychiatric Diagnostic Interviews for Children and Adolescents. *Child and Adolescent Psychiatry* 39 (1): 19–27.

McClellan, Jon M., and John Scott Werry. 2004. Evidence-Based Treatments in Child and Adolescent Psychiatry: An Inventory. *Child and Adolescent Psychiatry* 42 (12): 1388–1400.

Milgram, Stanley. 1974. *Obedience to Authority.* New York: Harper & Row.

Miller, William, and Stephen Rollnick. 1991. *Preparing People to Change Addictive Behavior.* New York: Guilford Press.

Montague, A., and F. Matson. 1979. *The Human Connection.* New York: McGraw-Hill.

Montaigne, Michel de. [1580] 1927. *On the Education of Children.* In E. Trechmann (Trans.), *Essays of Montaigne* (vol. 1 and 2). Milford, UK: Oxford University Press.

Montessori, Maria. [1912] 2002. *The Montessori Method.* Mineola, NY: Dover Publications.

Montgomery, M. 1997. The Powerlessness of Punishment: Angry Pride and Delinquent Identity. *Reclaiming Children and Youth* 6 (5): 162–166.

Murphy, Lois B., and Alice E. Moriarity. 1976. *Vulnerability, Coping, and Growth: From Infancy to Adolescence.* New Haven, CT: Yale University Press.

Neuwirth, Sharyn. 1993. *Learning Disabilities* (NIH Publication No. 93–3611). Bethesda, MD: National Institute of Mental Health. Available at www.kidsource.com/kidsource/content/learningdis.html (accessed October 20, 2005).

Nicholls, J. G. 1990. What Is Ability and Why Are We Mindful of It? A Developmental Perspective. In *Competence Considered,* edited by R. J. Sternberg and J. Kolligian, Jr., 11–40. New Haven, CT: Yale University Press.

Nouwen, Henri J. M. [1972] 1979. *The Wounded Healer.* New York: Image.

O'Connor, T. G., M. Rutter, and English and Romanian Adoptees Study Team. 2000. Attachment Disorder Behavior Following Early Severe Deprivation: Extension and Longitudinal Follow-Up. *Child and Adolescent Psychiatry* 39 (6): 703–712.

Parks, Alexia. 2002. *An American GULAG: Secret P.O.W. Camps for Teens.* Eldorado Springs, CO: The Education Exchange.

Patterson, G. R. 2002a. The Early Development of Coercive Family Processes. In *Antisocial Behavior in Children and Adolescents,* edited by John B. Reid, Gerald Patterson, and James Snyder, 25–44. Washington, DC: American Psychological Association.

Patterson, G. R. 2002b. Future Extensions of the Models. In *Antisocial Behavior in Children and Adolescents,* edited by John B. Reid, Gerald Patterson, and James Snyder, 273–283. Washington, DC: American Psychological Association.

Pennebaker, James. 1990. *Opening Up.* New York: Morrow.

Peterson, J. S. 2003. Listening: Resisting the Urge to Fix Them. In *Mentoring for Talent Development,* by Ken McCluskey and

Annabelle Mays, 126–142. Sioux Falls, SD: Reclaiming Youth
International.

Pfister, O. 1956. Therapy and Ethics in August Aichhorn's Treatment of
Wayward Youth. In *Searchlights on Delinquency*, edited by K. R.
Eisler, 35–49. New York: International Universities Press.

Provine, Robert. 2000. *Laughter: A Scientific Investigation*. New York:
Viking Press.

Rapaport, Anatol. 1960. *Fights, Games, and Debates*. Ann Arbor:
University of Michigan Press.

Raychaba, Brian. 1992. Doing and Being Done To. *Journal of Emotional
and Behavioral Problems* 1 (3): 4–9.

Raychaba, Brian. 1993. *Pain, Lots of Pain: Violence and Abuse in the
Lives of Young People in Care*. Ottawa, Canada: National Youth in
Care Network.

Redl, Fritz. [1957] 1966. *When We Deal With Children: Selected
Writings*. New York: Free Press.

Redl, Fritz. 1994. The Oppositional Child and the Confronting Adult: A
Mind to Mind Encounter. In *The Clinical Faces of Childhood* (vol.
1), edited by E. James Anthony and Doris G. Gilpin, 41–57.
Northvale, NJ: Jason Aronson, Inc.

Rohr, Richard. 1996. *Wild Man's Journey: Reflections on Male
Spirituality*. Cincinnati, OH: St. Anthony Messenger Press and
Franciscan Communications.

Ross-Kidder, Kathleen. 2002. *LD, ADHD and Delinquency: Is There a
Link?* Rockville, MD: National Joint Committee on Learning
Disabilities. Available at
www.ldonline.org0/ld_indepth/self_esteem/intro_delinquent. html
(accessed October 20, 2005).

Rotter, J. B. 1954. *Social Learning and Clinical Psychology*. Englewood
Cliffs, NJ: Prentice Hall.

Scales, Peter C., P. L. Benson, and Eugene C. Roehlkepartain. 2001.
*Grading Grown-Ups: American Adults Report on Their Real
Relationships with Kids*. Minneapolis, MN: Lutheran Brotherhood
and Search Institute.

Scheff, T. 1995. Self-Defense Against Verbal Assault: Shame, Anger, and
the Social Bond. *Family Process* 34: 271–286.

Search Institute. 1998. "Healthy Communities Healthy Youth Tool Kit."
Minneapolis, MN: Author. www.search-institute.org (accessed
October 13, 2005).

Seita, John, and Larry Brendtro. 2005. *Kids Who Outwit Adults.* Bloomington, IN: Solution Tree (formerly National Educational Service).

Seligman, Martin. 1992. *Helplessness: On Development, Depression and Death.* New York: W. H. Freeman.

Seligman, Martin, and C. Peterson. 2003. Positive Clinical Psychology. In *A Psychology of Human Strengths*, edited by L. G. Aspinwall and U. M. Staudinger, 305–318. Washington, DC: American Psychological Association.

Sells, Scott. 1998. *Treating the Tough Adolescent.* New York: Guilford Press.

Selye, Hans. 1978. *The Stress of Life* (rev. ed.). New York: McGraw Hill.

Shores, R., and J. Wehby. 1999. Analyzing the Classroom Social Behavior of Students with EBD. *Journal of Behavioral Disorders* 7 (4): 194–199.

Shure, M. 1992. *I Can Problem Solve (ICPS): An Interpersonal Cognitive Problem Solving Program* (preschool, kindergarten/primary, and intermediate grade eds.). Champaign, IL: Research Press.

Silber, Käte. 1973. *Pestalozzi: The Man and his Work* (3rd ed.). New York: Schocken Books.

Singer, Tanya, Ben Seymour, John O'Doherty, Holger Kaube, Raymond Dolan, and Chris Frith. 2004 (February 20). Empathy for Pain Involves the Affective but Not Sensory Components of Pain. *Science* 303 (5661): 1157–1162.

Skinner, B. F. 1989. *Recent Issues in the Analysis of Behavior.* Columbus, OH: Merrill.

Snyder, C. R., and Shane J. Lopez, eds. 2002. *Handbook of Positive Psychology.* New York: Oxford University Press.

Sternberg, Robert J. 1997. *Successful Intelligence.* New York: Plume Books.

Thompson, George, and Jerry B. Jenkins. 1993. *Verbal Judo: The Gentle Art of Persuasion.* New York: William Morrow.

Toch, Hans, and Kenneth Adams with J. Douglas Grant. 2002. *Acting Out: Maladaptive Behavior in Confinement.* Washington, DC: American Psychological Association.

Treffinger, D. 2003. The Role of Mentoring in Talent Development. In *Mentoring for Talent Development*, by K. McCluskey and A. Mays, 1–11. Sioux Falls, SD: Reclaiming Youth International.

Tutu, Desmond. 2002. Our Hope for the Future. In Brendtro, Brokenleg, and Van Bockern, *Reclaiming Youth at Risk*, ix–x.

Vanderven, Karen. 2000. Cultural Aspects of Point and Level Systems. *Reclaiming Children and Youth* 9 (1): 53–59.

Van Sant, Gus, director. 1998. *Good Will Hunting*. Miramax Films.

Varenhorst, Barbara. 2004. Tapping the Power of Peer Helping. *Reclaiming Children and Youth* 13 (3): 130–133.

Villa, Richard, and Jacqueline Thousand. 2000. *Restructuring for Caring and Effective Education*. Baltimore: Paul H. Brooks.

Viscott, David. 1996. *Emotional Resilience*. New York: Crown Publishers.

Vorrath, Harry, and Larry Brendtro. 1985. *Positive Peer Culture* (2nd ed.). New York: Aldine de Gruyter.

Vygotsky, Lev S. 1989. *Thought and Language*. Cambridge, MA: MIT Press.

Wachtel, T. 2003. Restorative Justice in Everyday Life: Beyond the Formal Ritual. *Reclaiming Children and Youth* 12 (2): 83–87.

Wagner, Mary M. 1995. Outcomes for Youths With Serious Emotional Disturbance in Secondary School and Early Adulthood. *The Future of Children: Critial Issues for Children and Youths* 5 (2): 90–112.

Waller, James. 2002. *Becoming Evil: How Ordinary People Commit Genocide and Mass Murder*. New York: Oxford University Press.

Walsh, Froma. 1998. *Strengthening Family Resilience*. New York: Guilford Press.

Wasmund, W., and Thomas Tate. 1995. *Partners in Empowerment*. Albion, MI: Starr Commonwealth.

Wasmund, W., and Thomas Tate. 1996. *Partners in Empowerment: A Peer Group Primer*. Albion, MI: Starr Commonwealth.

Werner, Emmy. 1995. Resilience and Development. *American Psychological Society* 4: 81–85.

Werner, Emmy, and Ruth Smith. 1992. *Overcoming the Odds: High Risk Children from Birth to Adulthood*. Ithaca, NY: Cornell University Press.

White, R. 1959. Motivation Reconsidered: The Concept of Competence. *Psychological Review* 66: 297–313.

Wilker, Karl. [1920] 1993. *Der Lindenhof*. Translated by Stephan Lhotzky. Sioux Falls, SD: Augustana College.

Willner, A., C. Braukmann, K. Kirigin, D. Fixsen, E. Phillips, and M. Wolf. 1970. The Training and Validation of Youth-Preferred Social Behaviors of Child-Care Personnel. *Journal of Applied Behavior Analysis* 10 (2): 219–230.

Wolin, Stephen J., and Sybil Wolin. 1993. *The Resilient Self: How Survivors of Troubled Families Rise Above Adversity.* New York: Villard.

Wood, Frank H. 1988. Factors in Intervention Choice. *Monograph in Behavioral Disorders* 11: 133–143. Arizona State University and Council for Children with Behavioral Disorders.

Zeigarnik, Bluma. 1927. Das Behalten von Erledigten und Unerledigten Handlungen [The Memory of Completed and Uncompleted Tasks]. *Psychologische Forschung* 9: 1–85.

Zillmann, D. 1993. Mental Control of Angry Aggression. In *Handbook of Mental Control*, edited by Daniel Wegner and James Pennebaker, 370–392. Upper Saddle River, NJ: Prentice-Hall.

Zimbardo, Phillip, C. Maslach, and C. Haney. 2002. Reflections on the Stanford Prison Experiment: Genesis, Transformations, Consequences. In *Obedience to Authority: Current Perspectives on the Milgram Paradigm*, edited by Thomas Blass, 193–237. Mahwah, NJ: Erlbaum.

Zins, J. E., ed. 2004. *Building Academic Success on Social and Emotional Learning: What Does the Research Say?* New York: Teachers College Press.

Strength-Based Training Opportunities

Reclaiming Youth conducts *Reclaiming Youth Seminars* in the United States and Canada and publishes the quarterly journal *Reclaiming Children and Youth*. It also operates a web-based bookstore and the Reclaiming Youth Speakers Bureau. Reclaiming Youth's mission is based on the Circle of Courage with Response Ability Pathways (RAP) providing core training in this approach.

Response Ability Pathways provides foundation skills for all who deal with young persons in the family, school, or community. Children and youth need supportive persons who *respond* to their needs rather than *react* to their problems. RAP provides these *response-abilities* that enable one to guide young persons on *pathways to responsibility*.

- *RAP applies Circle of Courage principles to meet growth needs of all young persons.* The goal is to provide children with opportunities to develop belonging, mastery, independence, and generosity.[1]

- *RAP methods are grounded in research evidence* on resilience, brain science, and positive youth development.[2]

- *RAP provides a powerful alternative to both punitive and permissive approaches.* Instead of reactive, coercive interactions, young persons are enlisted as responsible agents in positive change. RAP deals with problems by focusing on strengths and solutions.

- *RAP taps and develops the innate strength and resilience of young persons.* The course strengthens youth's ability to *connect* to others for support, *clarify* challenging problems, and *restore* harmony.

- *RAP is highly experiential and addresses the pressing challenges faced by all youth.* Basic RAP principles are enlivened by videos and small-group role-plays. Training leads to RAP certification, and credit for two semester hours can be arranged.

- *RAP training is built around "universal design" principles.* This ensures that training generalizes to work with children and youth in any setting:

- *RAP training is useful to all professionals and lay persons who deal with youth.* This course is highly rated by educators, counselors, social workers, psychologists, youth workers, and staff in treatment and juvenile justice settings. The skills also apply to parents, foster parents, and mature youth who are peer helpers or mentors.

For further information, please contact:

No Disposable Kids
Phone 1-800-315-5640
E-mail info@ndk.org
Visit www.ndk.org

Reclaiming Youth
Phone 1-800-647-5244
E-mail courage@reclaiming.com
Visit www.reclaiming.com

[1] RAP principles are drawn from the "Circle of Courage" model of positive youth development. See Brendtro, Brokenleg, and Van Bockern 2002.

[2] Brendtro and du Toit 2005. To maintain fidelity and facilitate evaluation, all RAP trainers are certified, and RAP is copyright and trademark-protected by the Circle of Courage.

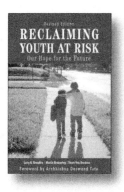

Reclaiming Youth at Risk: Our Hope for the Future

Larry K. Brendtro, Martin Brokenleg, and Steve Van Bockern

Foreword by Archbishop Desmond Tutu

Open new doors for youth at risk by using strategies based on a compelling, effective combination of Native American philosophies and Western psychology.

BKF116

Raising the Bar and Closing the Gap: Whatever It Takes

Richard DuFour, Rebecca DuFour, Robert Eaker, and Gayle Karhanek

This sequel to the best-selling *Whatever It Takes: How Professional Learning Communities Respond When Kids Don't Learn* expands on original ideas and presses further with new insights.

BKF378

Teaching Empathy: A Blueprint for Caring, Compassion, and Community

David A. Levine

This resource focuses on teaching empathy and building a culture of caring in the classroom. A CD of the author's original music enhances the learning experience.

BKF202

Reclaiming Youth At Risk: Our Hope for the Future

Larry K. Brendtro, Martin Brokenleg, and Steve Van Bockern

Venture inside schools that have successfully reached youth at risk. Set includes three 20-minute DVDs and a facilitator's guide.

DVF011

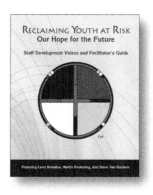